Art and Children

Using Literature to Expand Creativity

by
Robin W. Davis

School Library Media, No. 9

The Scarecrow Press, Inc.
Lanham, Md., and London
1996

SCARECROW PRESS, INC.

Published in the United States of America
by Scarecrow Press, Inc.
4720 Boston Way
Lanham, Maryland 20706

4 Pleydell Gardens, Folkestone
Kent CT20 2DN, England

British Cataloguing-in-Publication Information Available

Library of Congress Cataloging-in-Publication Data

Davis, Robin Works, 1962–
Art and children : using literature to expand creativity / by Robin W. Davis.
p.   cm. — (School library media series ; no. 9)
Includes bibliographical references and index.
1. Art—Study and teaching (Early childhood) 2. Literature—Study
and teaching (Early childhood) 3. Early childhood education—Activity
programs.   I. Title.   II. Series.
LB1139.5.A78D39   1996   372.5′044—dc20   96-18941   CIP
ISBN 0–8108–3158–9 (pbk. : alk. paper)

♾ TM The paper used in this publication meets the minimum requirements of
American National Standard for Information Sciences—Permanence of Paper
for Printed Library Materials, ANSI Z39.48–1984.
Manufactured in the United States of America.

Contents

Part III   Exploring: From Art to Book

Editor's Foreword

The School Library Media Series is directed to the school library media specialist, particularly the building level librarian. The multifaceted role of the librarian as educator, collection developer, curriculum developer and information spe- cialist is examined. The series includes concise, practical books on topical and current subjects related to programs and services.

Integration of visual arts within the primary school curriculum is the focus of *Art and Children: Using Literature to Expand Creativity*. Current works, primarily picture books, can be used to illustrate various artistic techniques.

This book contains an interesting section that explores the relationship of the arts to cognitive and social development. An art activity related to the theme of each picture book is provided.

Diane de Cordova Biesel
Series Editor

Introduction

Beautiful and interesting children's books can be used as motivation to encourage creativity, self expression, and artistic development in children. Books can help children closely experience art. Various artistic methods and techniques can also be experienced through literature. And what better way to teach a child abstract notions such as imagination and vision than through a book that can be read and reread? Artists and illustrators of children's books are sensitive and aware of the child's view of the world. The pictures in these books can teach art appreciation in all its aspects.

This book is designed for the practicing early childhood educator, teacher, or librarian who is interested in helping young children to reach their artistic potential and retain creativity. Those working with children through age eight will find the information helpful, useful, and fun.

Art plays a vital role in early childhood education. It provides a means for interpreting and expressing human experience as well as imparting cognitive information. A child's natural state of mind is creative and artistic. But there are pressures placed on children in school that can "kill" creativity. Most young children beginning kindergarten love exploring creativity. By the time they reach the third grade, much of their enthusiasm and pleasure has dissipated. Dr. Teresa Amabile, creativity specialist, has put together a list of creativity killers that commonly occur:

- **Surveillance:** constant observation that destroys risk taking in artistic ventures.
- **Evaluation:** judging the "quality" of a child's creation.

- **Rewards:** excessive use of prizes for art done the "right" way.
- **Competition:** putting kids in a win-lose situation, such as art contests.
- **Over-control:** using work sheets or copying art work instead of allowing artistic license.
- **Restricting choice:** not allowing children free access to art and creative materials every day.
- **Time limits:** stopping a child in the middle of the creative process.

Self-esteem is tied to creativity. Self esteem and the creative powers are at their peak in the preschool child. As soon as a child is placed in a structured, traditional setting, there is a sharp drop in both self-esteem and creativity.

By integrating art throughout a child's day these creativity killers can be counteracted. By allowing children to become totally absorbed in a project, to slowly savor art all through each subject, by not judging or restricting, creativity can be enhanced.

The emphasis of this book is not on art as philosophy, but on art as an integral and strengthening part of the curriculum. Its goal is to aid in the teaching of concepts in such areas as math, science, social studies, reading, language arts, music and drama in an enjoyable and unique manner. Regardless of your previous artistic experience, this curriculum can be a rewarding experience.

Sources

Amabile, Teresa. *Growing Up Creative: A Lifetime of Creativity*. Creative Education Foundation, 1992.

Part I

Learning: Art and Children

1

Integrating Art Information and Literature for Children

"It is possible to teach reading through a program of instruction primarily focused on the arts." This was demonstrated through a series of programs in New York public schools put on by the Solomon R. Guggenheim Museum titled "Learning to Read Through the Arts." (See *Beyond Creating: The Place for Art in America's Schools,* Getty Center for Education in the Arts, 1985.) The focus was on both the reading and artistic aspects of the program. This type of focus fits well into what research has shown us about the way children learn to read.

Reading is viewed by the specialists as a dynamic, child-based process, with real experiences taking the place of phonics and skill drills. Many books of literature-based activities are available, and the teaching of content areas through literature is a popular method. Art can also be connected with literature and can infiltrate the entire curriculum by using a multimedia, multisensory approach. By using an area of high interest and success for this age level, adults can further stimulate learning and establish a focus for developing academic skills. Art is just such a high-interest area.

Even though teachers and librarians have many things that they must consider, arts must be included in the curriculum in order to nuture self-esteem and creativity. Art can also aid teachers in helping children reach the national education goals set forth in George Bush's "America 2000" education strategy. Artistic activities coordinated with classroom subjects can range from books and audiovisuals, to displays, demonstrations, and festivals. The arts can enable us to realize our humanity. Through them children can learn to interpret and express their behavior and experiences.

These ideas are especially important in early childhood, where children are still forming their self-concept. If children begin to experience art, creative activities, and literature in early elementary programs, they are more likely to continue on this path for the remainder of their lives. With a literature-based art program, these ideas can be accomplished. Art can be studied through literature in terms of its history, outstanding artists, and illustration methods. Aesthetics can also be presented through the relationship between art and text. Several versions of stories can be shown to demonstrate contrasts and comparisons among artists' interpretations of the text. Art styles can also be studied and explained using with current picture book illustrations.

Using art in the curriculum also emphasizes "sensory" learning. The young child continually uses all of his/her senses to gain knowledge of the world and to develop language. Because sensory learning is so important, children in an art-related curriculum learn experientially, doing things first-hand. It is not enough to tell them about a painting. They must see it, hold a paintbrush, smell the paint, feel the textured canvas, and listen to the words of the artist. In this way, all the senses are involved. It is through interaction with an object or piece of knowledge that it is learned.

A unit approach works well when integrating art into the curriculum. Units are organized around a theme, such as clay and pottery, or focused on a particular book. Each unit is planned for a day, a week, or longer depending on the interest level and time limitations of the group of children. Each activity the children experience relates to the theme under study.

A "web" is a good way to plan a unit with an art focus. First, write the theme in the center of a blank paper and brainstorm all of the terms, ideas, and concepts you can think of. Write these in a web formation around your main theme. Specific activities are added as the web is refined and adapted. Next, a general plan of activities is written for a selected time frame. A sample general plan on the topic of "Clay and Pottery" follows.

Clay and Pottery

Examples of picture books about clay and pottery

Baylor, Byrd. *When Clay Sings*. Charles Scribner's Sons, 1972.

Dixon, Annabelle. *Clay*. Garrett, 1990.

Drummond, Allan. *The Willow Pattern Story*. North South, 1992.

Engle, Diana. *The Little Lump of Clay*. Morrow, 1989.

Florian, Douglas. *A Potter*. Greenwillow, 1991.

Gibbons, Gail. *The Pottery Place*. HBJ, 1987.

Jameson, Cynthia. *The Clay Pot Boy*. Coward McCann, 1973.

Rehnman, Mats. *Clay Flute*. F, S, & G, 1989.

Books about how to model clay

Hull, Jeannie. *Clay*. Watts, 1989.

Kohl, MaryAnn. *Mudworks: Creative Clay, Dough, and Modeling Experiences*. Bright Ring, 1989.

O'Reilly, Susie. *Modeling*. Thompson Learning, 1993.

Owen, Annie. *The Modeling Book*. Simon and Schuster, 1990.

Roussel, Mike. *Clay*. Rourke, 1990.

Artists to study

Fowler, Carol. *Daisy Hooee Nampeyo*. Dillon, 1977.

Nelson, Mary Carroll. *Maria Martinez*. Dillon, 1972.

Swentzell, Rina. *Children of Clay: A Family of Pueblo Potters*. Lerner, 1992.

Objectives

1. To experience forming an object with a solid material.
2. To connect touching with mental images.
3. To learn manipulative skills in shaping clay.

Related Vocabulary

Wedging, porcelain, stoneware, slip, glaze, clay, pottery, molding, firing.

Clay is a very kinesthetically satisfying medium. It is also a great interactive activity. Children seated together can talk as their art takes shape and form through their hands. Although it can be messy, its benefits far outweigh this one drawback. Working with clay fosters large muscle and fine motor control. Children enjoy it, for it has the appeal of "playing in the mud" for them. It also allows the flexibility to change or undo what has been done much easier than is the case with drawing or painting. Children can control the medium. Clay, with its distinct texture, color, and smell, is multisensory. Making homemade clay lends itself to a lesson in measuring, reading, and mixing ingredients. Clay needs lots of kneading to keep it pliable. It should also be kept moist and sealed in airtight containers. With the children, get to know the clay by rolling, squeezing, coiling, flattening, pinching, pounding, poking, cutting, stamping, twisting, and bending. Use objects such as toothpicks, pipe cleaners, buttons, sticks, shells, and nails to decorate a clay sculpture.

Sources of clay:

ABC School Supply
General Catalog
3312 N. Berkeley Lane
P.O. Box 100019
Duluth, GA 30136
1-800-669-4ABC

American Art Clay Company
4717 West 16th Street
Indianapolis, IN 46222

Reading and Language Arts

- Discuss and display objects made from clay, using *Clay* by Dixon.
- Share the story *The Pottery Place* by Gibbons.

Social Studies

- Share the book *Children of Clay* by Swentzell. Do a mini-study on the Pueblo Indians and their culture, including maps and history.

  Some books to use:

  Arnold, Caroline. *The Ancient Cliff Dwellers of Mesa Verde*. Clarion, 1992.

  D'Apice, Mary. *The Pueblo*. Rourke, 1990.

  Keegan, Marcia. *Pueblo Boy: Growing Up in Two Worlds*. Cobblehill/Dutton, 1991.

  Yue, Charlotte. *The Pueblo*. Houghton Mifflin, 1986.

Math

- Use a scale to weigh both wet and dry clay. Which is heavier?
- Weigh different types of clay: Earthenware, Porcelain, Stoneware.

• Measure a pot before and after it dries. Is there a difference? Do the same before firing.

Science

• Do different tests on a clay object: tap it, feel it, scratch it, break it. Record the sensory results on a chart.
• Discuss, show and define the types of clay: Porcelain, Stoneware, Earthenware.
• Discuss the concepts of wet and dry.
• Do a waterproof test: soak a china mug and a clay pot in water. Which one absorbs, and which one repels?
• Put three tablespoons of soil into a jar of water. After a few days, it will be separated into a layer of clay and one of dirt. The clay is the top layer.

Music and Drama

• Use these action rhymes: "Here's a Piece of Modeling Clay," from *Twiddling Your Thumbs: Hand Rhymes* by Wendy Cope (Faber and Faber, 1988, page 19); "I Stretch It, I Pound It," from *Favorite Fingerplays and Action Rhymes* by Gratia Kahle (Dennison, 1987, page 13).
• Do Reader's Theater with the book *When Clay Sings* by Baylor. Each column or paragraph can be a part for a child. Use stick puppets or masks traced from designs found in the book if desired.
• Play music from the Pueblos from *American Indian Songs and Chants* by the Bala Sinem Choir (Silo Music, 1990).

- Read aloud the book *The Spider, the Cave and the Pottery Bowl* by Eleanor Clymer. Adapt the story into a play for your class to perform.

Culminating Activity

Use the book *When Clay Sings* by Baylor. Demonstrate the coil pot technique that the Indian women are doing on page nine. First, make a pinch pot. A pinch pot is made by using a ball of clay of the desired size. Stick both thumbs in the center with your fingers holding the outside. Gently press your thumbs against the sides while pinching and rotating the clay. Continue until the desired shape is formed. Now, roll long snakes of clay out on a flat surface. Wrap the coils of clay on the outside of the pinch pot. You may smooth over the creases if desired. Carve on your pot some of the designs shown in the book, or paint them on after it is dry. Let the children repeat this process after your demonstration.

2

Relationship of the Arts to Cognitive and Social Development

An art-integrated curriculum brings a child into contact with a variety of materials and sensory experiences. These experiences are utilized by the teacher to reach educational goals. Sometimes the goals will be artistic, at other times, social or cognitive. For example, the arts offer a wide range of new vocabulary to share with children. The names of colors, shapes, materials, tools, techniques, and methods are introduced. Other general cognitive, social, and creative content area goals are

Reading and Language Arts

- Develop ability to communicate with others verbally and non-verbally, through art talks and sharing.
- Practice listening skills, through directions for projects.
- Develop appreciation of good literature, through the introduction of books.
- Expand vocabulary.

11

- Promote fluency of expression in many forms.
- Understand the meaning of pictures and written language, through stories, art works, recipes, and other activities.
- Practice thinking, problem solving, and discovery.

Science and Social Studies

- Discover the joy of life and expression through the plastic arts.
- Promote cooperation through group art activities.
- Communicate ideas through listening, speaking, reading, and presenting ideas in graphic form.
- Foster the values of friendship and cooperation through group projects.
- Promote self-understanding and acceptance.
- Locate, gather and evaluate ideas for projects.
- Discover that the senses help us learn.
- Interpret graphic material.
- Improve critical thinking skills through aesthetics.
- Learn about shape, color, form, texture, and other art elements.

Math

- Balance concepts with skills and abilities.
- Emphasize the thinking process and concept development.
- Introduce graphs and symbols.
- Perceive, describe, and extend patterns.

- Develop comparison and classification skills.
- Develop ordering, counting, and measuring skills.

Music and Drama

- Develop large and small muscles and eye-hand coordination.
- Provide tactile, manipulation, and coordination experience.
- Offer emotional release.
- Encourage feeling and verbalizing.
- Gain self-confidence as a member of the group.
- Develop auditory skills.
- Communicate through dramatization.

Art also develops . . .

- The child's awareness of internal responses to external stimuli in the environment.
- A child's competence and skills needed to make art.
- A child's awareness of cultural heritage through art history.
- Artistic judgment and standards.
- Basic information about color, texture, line, space, perspective, technique and other design concepts.
- A child's understanding of the world through exposure to the different ways of seeing and making art.
- Creative potential in all areas and encourages experimentation in creativity.
- Personal artistic style.
- Physical and manipulative activity, as well as relaxation, through painting, cutting, pasting. Eye-hand coordination is also an important outcome of experiences with art.

- Flexibility, experimentation, and involvement with ideas.
- Cognitive development. Intellectual concepts are learned in every art project.

To teach this	Use books that illustrate such ideas as
Reading and Language Arts	Illustrated Alphabets Picture Dictionaries Plays or drama
History	Architecture Costume Heraldry
Math	Graphs and graph pictures Cooking Tangrams Geometry Shadows and time Patterns
Science	Photographs Nature Colors Texture
Social Studies	Self portraits Family portraits Art from other cultures Historical events
Music	Song books Musical literature

Objectives of a literature-based art program for early childhood are:

1. To involve students in and expose them to beautiful art work and wonderful literature.
2. To expose children to the variety of ways artists have expressed themselves and to different artistic styles.
3. To let the children work with a wide variety of art materials.
4. To promote sensory education and pleasure through work with various materials and media.
5. To express feelings, emotions, or story interpretations through various art activities.
6. To develop fine hand-eye coordination and motor development through various art activities.
7. To learn self-respect and appreciation through artistic accomplishment.
8. To promote reading and children's literature.
9. To enhance language development.
10. To encourage curiosity and creativity.
11. To let children learn through all of their senses.
12. To use art to determine each child's best learning modality (visual, auditory, or kinesthetic) in order to teach them in the most effective manner.
13. To teach the other curricular areas in a way children will like and enjoy.

A Note about Whole Language

A Whole-Language approach to teaching involves children in all modes of communication: reading, writing, listening, observing, and speaking. The activities that are used to introduce children to the visual arts fit well into this approach because art is another form of communication. The activities and ideas in this book can be used as part of a Whole-Language reading program or as part of an art-based program that has the secondary benefit of exposing children to literature. There are many different definitions of what constitutes a Whole-Language program. What Whole Language suggests is that children learn to read by being provided with many ways to use, interact with, and have power over language. The idea is that the connection between reading and language acquisition is very close. Whole Language makes heavy use of children's literature, using whole language and whole literature with whole children. Whole Language has several practices that are in support of its approach, all of which can easily be used in an art-based curriculum:

- Children acquire language through actually using it in its whole original context, not as a set of separate skill and drill exercises.
- Children read or are read to constantly, and are immersed in a literature-rich environment. In a classroom or library setting, this means literature is integrated throughout the program.
- Familiar stories are used repeatedly so that the child can get to know language intimately. New materials are also used to constantly expand the child's exposure to language.
- Children are allowed to communicate with language in many ways. This includes listening, speaking, reading, writing, and artistically interpreting language.

- Whole Language is integrated, child-centered, active, full of meaning, full of response, full of sharing, and natural.

3

Identifying Artistically Talented Children

The following list will help you in identifying talent in the visual arts in a fair and quick way. The artistic child:

- Enjoys other creative activities such as reading or imagining.
- Has outstanding sensitivity to the environment.
- Is competitive.
- Admires artists and artistic teachers.
- Prefers an art career.
- Spends a lot of time doing art.
- Uses imagination, daydreaming and storytelling in his/her art.
- Is willing to alter his/her art work to improve it.
- Is aware that others recognize his/her talents.
- Has original ideas.
- Uses complexity and detail in art.
- Is sensitive to line, color, shape, texture, etc.
- Responds to artistic peers.
- Possesses a high level of curiosity.
- Likes to experiment and take risks.

4

Creative Products from an Art/Literature Curriculum

Advertisements
Annotated bibliography
  (with illustrations)
Art gallery
Batik
Blueprint
Board game
Book making
Bulletin board
Card game
Cartoon
Ceramics
Charcoal sketch
Coins
Collage
Collection (with illustra-
  tions)
Comic strip
Commercial story board
Computer animation
Costume
Dance

Demonstration
Diagram
Diary (illustrated)
Diorama
Display
Drama
Etching
Experiment record
Fable
Fairy tale
Family tree
Filmstrip
Flash cards
Game
Graph
Greeting card
Haiku
Illustration
Invention
Journal
Labeled diagram
Large-scale drawing

Letter
Map
Maze
Mobile
Model
Movie
Mural
Museum exhibit
Music
Newspaper
Oil painting
Package for a product
Pamphlet
Pantomime
Pattern
Photograph
Picture dictionary
Pictograph
Play
Poem
Poster
Pottery
Puppet
Puppet show
Puzzle

Readers' theater
Recipe
Replica
Rubbing
Salt map
Sand casting
Scrapbook
Sculpture
Shadow box
Silk screen
Slide presentation
Song
Stencil
Stitchery
Story center
Tape recording
Terrarium
Time line
Transparency
Travelogue
TV newscast
Video tape
Watercolor painting
Work sheet

5

Stages in Children's Artistic Development

Basic Ideas

Children display a course of artistic progression that can be observed through their artwork. This course generally goes from scribbles to discernible images to symbolic representations. Although we can identify this sequence of development, each child moves through the stages differently. There is considerable variation among individual children due to their environment as well as other factors. What follows is a general overview of artistic development based on the research of Kellogg, Lowenfield, and Brittain.

Stage One: Scribbling and Mark Making (birth to two and up)

Nonverbal self-expression is present in the very young child through scribbling and mark making. These youngsters are

This lively drawing by a four-year-old reveals the way in which preschool children play with lines and shapes as they experiment with the use of symbols. Meandering and radiating lines combine with circular forms to suggest people. Notice how lines also are used to form the artist's name, "Matt."

exploring their arm and hand movements as well as their writing tool. Scribbling is the baby gibberish of art work. These children do not and cannot depict real images. Scribbling and mark making are done for pleasure, and are random and uncontrolled. The whole hand is used to grip the writing tool, and these children may not even look at the paper as they mark. Lines are more important than colors at this stage.

Stage Two:
Personal Symbols and Designs
(two to four and up)

Reality emerges from the child's vocabulary of marks at this stage. Scribbles, marks, shapes, and lines all represent something to the child, and are often named by the child. A circle and a line might represent "Mommy." To help children with this stage, let them manipulate lots of art-making materials and avoid using coloring books. The children have better control of tools than in Stage One and draw with variety, but they have a short attention span. Basic shapes come easier with improved motor control.

Stage Three:
Representational
(four to seven and up)

Children at this stage have a significantly different way of representing ideas artistically. Once kids realize that drawing can be symbolic, they begin to customize the symbols used in Stage Two. These children can show perspective and dimension, although sometimes not proportional. They are quite imaginative! Attention is paid to detail and design. At this stage, art is still personal self-expression, although they may be moving towards a product-focused orientation.

Providing for Young Children's Developmental Needs in Artistic Activities

Characteristic	Providing for the Characteristic
They are very active.	Art activities that do not require long periods of sitting.
They are egocentric.	Use art activities that build the child's self-image.
Children have varying levels of physical development.	Allow for individual outcomes to projects.
They do not yet have fully developed visual and auditory skills.	Use large pictures and print.
They learn through play.	Provide a wealth of materials and activities.
They do not always distinguish between fantasy and reality.	Experiment and allow them imaginative activities.

6

Some Basic Art Concepts

Line

Lines are part of every piece of art and are everywhere in the environment. Lines may be straight, curved, wavy, zigzag, or broken. Lines can be formed into symbols or letters. All lines have a beginning, middle, and end. The book *Look Again* by Tana Hoban (New York: Macmillan, 1971) is a good example of lines found in our world. Explore lines in art by placing a piece of clear acetate over an art reproduction. Have the children trace with a marker on to the acetate the lines they see in the artwork. Discuss the types of lines discovered.

Shape

Shape covers two-dimensional space. Shape can represent real or imagined objects, made from a line that encloses itself. Shapes are geometric or irregular, filled, empty, or

---

For an in depth look at the concept of color, see part three.

overlapping. Shapes can be of any size. There are squares, circles, triangles, octagons, hexagons, spheres, and others. *First Shapes* by Ivan and Jane Chermayeff (New York: Abrams, 1991) and *Shape* by Philip Yenawine (New York: Delacorte/MOMA, 1991) are two excellent books on shape. Explore shape by photocopying a reproduction. Instruct the children to color in all the different shapes they see formed in the art.

Texture

Texture is the visual depiction of how things feel, or the surface quality of a real object. Texture is related primarily to touching. Texture can be descibed as soft, slimy, puffy, sticky, prickly, and more. Use the book *Is It Rough? Is It Smooth? Is It Shiny?* by Tana Hoban (New York: Greenwillow, 1984). Explore texture by making texture art. Cut designs from tissue paper. Gather up scraps of netting, glitter, foil, fabric, cardboard, and paper. Use white glue to attach these different textures into a pleasant design.

Design or composition

Design is the organization of space in an artwork. A design is like a blueprint or a plan for the art. Design is the way the color, line, shape, and other elements are placed. Designs have repetition, balance, rhythm, unity, or variety.

Light

Light makes us able to see all of the elements of art. Value is the light or dark quality of a particular color. *Color and Light* by David Evans (London: Dorling Kindersley, 1993) is a good resource. Demonstrate light source by shining a flashlight on a ball from behind, above, below, etc. Point out where the shadows fall.

7

Planning Art Experiences
for Children

Good guidance in an art-related curriculum begins with good planning. All art activities should be planned with the educational goals and needs of the children in mind. An interesting array of activities should be arranged before the children arrive. A variety of art materials should be available daily. Projects should be rotated regularly, or variations added to them. The projects should address creating art, looking at art, and living with art. Projects in these three categories have the following elements:

Creating Art
- Ideas for art
- Utilizes design skills
- Utilizes creativity
- Introduces media, proceses, and tools.

Looking at Art
- Perception and vocabulary of art
- Aesthetics or judging art
- Artistic styles
- Art history

Living with Art
- Visual awareness exercises
- Artists and art careers
- Local art places, such as museums and galleries
- Art and design in everyday life

The early childhood art program will provide the time and the place to express a child's feelings through various media. There are four ideas to emphasize, the first of which is to high-light the *process* of making art, and not the end product. During the process, the feelings are experienced, and the expression of self is the most important aspect of a child's art. The program should also meet the developmental needs of the children as mentioned earlier, in "Stages in Children's Artistic Development." That means it should be appropriate to the age, ability, and interests of the children. The program should also give the child a chance for originality and creative thinking, and allow the child to create at his or her own artistic pace.

Presentation of Activities

The success of the art activities you present will greatly depend on how they are presented. What is needed is a teacher who is aware of his/her own interests and skills that can be utilized in the art activities. The teacher must also be well prepared. Art activities should be modeled for the children, and therefore practiced before they are presented. Consider the following when presenting an art idea:

- The objectives of the activity
- What can be learned from the activity

- What materials are needed
- What is the best room or table set up for the activity
- Determine how to stimulate the participants' interest throughout the activity
- Anticipate the children's questions
- Plan a way to evaluate the activity
- Consider any appropriate follow-up activities
- Consider clean-up time and materials

Be prepared! This is perhaps the most important rule when planning an art activity. As mentioned, practice the activity physically if possible before presenting it to the children. Make sure that all needed equipment is present and in working order. Read any directions completely before doing the activity. Activities may be modified if necessary to meet the needs of particular children. Prearrange the materials so they will be easy to distribute. Explain and pass out materials, using as little time as possible. After the children begin, be sure to move among them and offer suggestions or answer questions.

Setting Up for Art Activities

Whether you have a small corner or an entire room, there are basic guidelines to be followed for arranging the environment. Age group should always be a major consideration in planning. Other basic considerations are:

1. Set up the area for ease of dispensing and cleaning up of materials.
2. Sharp objects or wet materials should be out of the reach of children who have not mastered their handling.

3. If there is no sink in the area, a plastic kitchen tub half filled with water works well; supply plenty of paper towels.
4. Other materials should be arranged at a level where children can help themselves.
5. An area should be set aside for drying of paintings or other art works. A clothes line or drying rack can be used.
6. Set up materials so that children can have daily art experiences. Have something available, even if it is just crayons and paper.
7. The art area should facilitate the children's creative experiences. This means a predictable, organized, but accessible and fun area.

Art Learning Centers

The place in which an art-related curriculum occurs should have several activity areas called Art Learning Centers. The learning center is a small area of the room where an activity is set up. This idea can be traced back to the work of such educators as Johann Pestalozzi, who believed that children learn through direct interaction with each other and their environment. Children can use several of the learning centers throughout the day in periods of self-selected activity. They are allowed to move freely among the centers, which all have educational worth.

The learning centers need to be filled with non-structured art activities that leave wide latitude for interpretation and enjoyment. Plain paper is preferable to coloring sheets. Materials should also be suited to the topic or theme of the day.

Good guidance for the art activities means having all materials organized and ready to be used. Plan time for the completion of entire projects. Allow for unique and individual creations by making no models or filling in the color work sheets.

An art program such as this encourages creativity by giving children many opportunities to play, experiment, and discover as they engage in activities that help with problem-solving and conceptual skills. Be sure and leave time for individual expression through experimentation and nonstructured activity in the learning centers. Think of the art activity as pre-reading or -writing experiences. Teachers might find it helpful to keep an "idea book" of activities, art work, and sources of inspiration at each art center. Interesting photos or pictures can be added as you come across them while browsing through magazines or other sources. Children can also be encouraged to look through the book when they are at a loss for ideas while working at a learning center.

Children in preschool through age eight are emerging from the scribble stage of art. These children love to express themselves through drawings and paintings using bright colors, with large pencils or brushes and lots of extra paper. The content of their art typically relates to the children themselves and to their families. At this age range, the appropriate materials are paint, pencils, markers, crayons, clay, yarn, string, blocks, chalk and sand. Students are capable of exploring line, shape, color, form and texture, using both two- and three-dimensional methods. Two rules for a teacher or librarian to follow are: never dictate an art project and never do the child's art for him/her. If a child is unable or unwilling to do a project, it is simply the wrong activity for that child at that time. Art must be voluntary, and one of several choices made available. Forcing a child to do art or imitate another's art is likely to inhibit natural development and undermine self-esteem. The teacher serves as an observer and resource person in the art process. The teacher plans the activity, prepares the environment, selects the materials, leads sharing times, and responds individually to the children's art. The making of the art must be left to the child.

Other Ideas

- To help with self-esteem and identity, have an "Art Circle Time." This is a show-and-tell time for children to share the art work that they have created during the week. Set aside a regular time for this, and thank each child for sharing. This should be a positive, encouraging experience. Matting and displaying children's art work also adds a feeling of value. Art can be displayed on a wall, shelf, window or other area. Matte board scraps can be obtained from a frame shop. Boxes, styrofoam trays, or pie tins are other materials to use as frames. Make sure the children sign their work in a visible spot, or label the work with a small card next to it.
- An art party is a way to involve parents in a celebration of children's art. Sample art from each child can be displayed on his/her desk or seating area. As part of the program, tell the parents or give them a handout on how art and creativity are used throughout your program.
- Have easels equipped with large brushes, lots of paper, and a clear floor space covered with newspaper ready at all times.
- Push together some tables in a semicircle and put clay, cardboard, and water containers on them. Also include lots of manipulative equipment such as rolling pins,

spoons, toothpicks, and cookie cutters. Do the same for a set of tables that feature collage materials such as glue, sequins, feathers, scrap paper, beads, and yarn. The semicircle arrangement allows for social interaction during art play.

- Have a small stepladder in the area to crawl on and look at things from different views.
- Make a castle or house out of cardboard boxes. Let the children design and construct the building, from blueprint to painting. Hang children's art work inside and call it your "museum" or "gallery."
- A variety of materials and equipment is important. Some children who do not respond to more frequently presented art activities are attracted to unexpected ones. New mediums, such as pastels, paper mosaic, potato printing, or rubbings, can be introduced. Using alternative materials such as sand, earth, leaves, flowers, and cookie dough are other ideas.
- Create an interest table. Found objects, works of art, aquariums, and unusual man-made and exotic forms can be used. This is an area in which children can look closely and develop visual sensitivity.
- Establish an art library with books and prints for the children to use.
- Create an "Art Is Everywhere" area—use a bulletin board to show ever-changing examples of commercial art, photographs, packages, ads, and natural objects.
- A still-life corner should be provided to aid in realistic drawing experiences. Objects such as bottles, cloth, sticks, bones, plants, and fruit can be found in this area.
- Pictures can be read just as books are read, so use lots of "visual props." If visual props are appropriate, attractive, and accessible, children will read a creative message into them. Hang visuals at a child's eye-level and group them

in attractive patterns. Label art works and hang them close to a related book or activity area. Display visual props by gluing pictures to a roller blind and unroll a little each day. Visual props do not mean a major investment. There are many sources for free or inexpensive visuals, including used magazines, parents, or the child's own art.

Safety

Some art supplies contain harmful toxins. When purchasing materials, choose products that are clearly labeled with "Conforms to ASTM D-4236" (a federal standard). Always work with art materials in a well-ventilated area. Make sure that children do not eat or drink in the art area, that they wash their hands, and do not put art tools in their mouths. Obtain the list "Art and Craft Materials Acceptable for Kindergarten and Grades 1–6" from the California Department of Health Services, Center for the Safety in the Arts, 5 Beekman Street, New York, NY 10038. Phone: (212)227-6220. Cost is $5.00.

Materials List

These materials can easily be found at home or from a local crafts store. An excellent mail order source for supplies is:
   Dick Blick
   POB 1267
   Galesburg, IL 61402-1267
   1-800-447-8192

Painting

Brushes or items like brayers, rolling pins, toy cars, deodor-
    ant bottles
Plastic lids, coasters, pie pans, as palettes
Plastic bowls, muffin tins, or egg cartons to hold paint
Sponges
Plastic squeeze bottles
Newsprint paper
60 lb. drawing paper
Watercolor paper
Paint (Tempera, finger paint, oil, acrylic, watercolor, gouache)
Inverted egg cartons with holes punched, to hold wet brushes

Clay and Pottery

Covered plastic pail or airtight coffee can for wet clay
    storage
Moist clay
Tongue depressors or sticks
Thick-gauge wire
Tools for modeling clay (coat hangers, nails, plastic spoons,
    forks, knives, etc.)
Rolling pin

Drawing

Pencils (varying softness of lead)
Chalk
Pastels
Crayons
Colored pencils

Markers
Drawing paper of various textures

Collage

Staplers
Glue
Scissors
Paper punches
Brushes for glue (use synthetic bristle)
Tape
Magazines to cut
Material scraps
Yarn or string
Tissue paper
Wall paper
Cellophane (various colors)
Corrugated cardboard
Dried grass, bark, leaves
Feathers

Weaving, Fiber, and Fabric

Yarn
Fabric scraps
Straws
Heavy cardboard
Large-eye rug needles
Masking tape
Scissors
Shoe boxes for looms

Ribbon
Beads
Dried leaves, grass, plants
India ink
White glue

Printmaking

Newspaper
Water-based ink
Cardboard
Popsicle sticks
Cookie sheets
White drawing paper

Clean-Up

Buckets
Sponges
Detergent
Newspapers
Aprons

Also . . .

An iron
A drying rack or clothesline and pins
Food coloring
Blueprint paper
Flat boxes for art storage

8

Looking at Art: Aesthetics

Aesthetics is the appreciation of beauty. Aesthetics uses all the senses as well as the imagination. Although young children do not make mature artistic judgments, they can respond aesthetically and benefit from experiences with art.

To develop an aesthetic sense in children, help them seek out beauty and wonder in their world. The purpose is simply to add to the richness and fullness of their lives. Aesthetic experiences are chosen according to the child's interest and developmental level. A variety of experiences, visual, auditory, and kinesthetic, should be offered.

The environment plays a special part in developing the aesthetic sense. Enhance the environment with soft, neutral colors. This will allow works of visual art to stand out. Use the following activities to expand aesthetic awareness.

"Do You See What I See?"

Have the group look at a particular art work for about 30 seconds. A good one to use is Vincent Van Gogh's *Starry Night*. Remove the image and ask some questions. What was in the painting? What colors? Are there any people in the painting? Turn the painting around and study it longer. Ask the group what they see now. How does the painting make you feel? What do you like or dislike about the painting? Why? These kinds of questions will help children to see and to be aware of their responses to art. The questions could be used with any other piece of art.

Telescoping

Visual perceptiveness is a skill used in looking at a painting, reading a book, or even doing a math problem. Roll up and tape $4'' \times 6''$ index cards into tubes. Have the children examine different parts of a painting through the tubes and describe what they see.

Styles

Children can be made aware of particular book illustration styles. For example, use books by Leo Lionni. Children can then make their own torn paper animal collages and experience how the art was made.

Art Prints for Appreciation

Use prints of the following to share with children
Paul Cézanne   *Apples and Oranges*

Leonardo Da Vinci	*Mona Lisa*
Edgar Dégas	*Dancer and Bouquet*
Edouard Manet	*The Boat*
Henri Matisse	*Goldfish*
Jean Millet	*Feeding Her Birds*
Georgia O'Keeffe	*Black Iris*
Pablo Picasso	*Child with Dove*
Jackson Pollock	*Mural*
Pierre-Auguste Renoir	*Girl with a Watering Can*
Henri Rousseau	*Jungle, Setting Sun*
Georges Seurat	*La Grande Jatte*
Vincent Van Gogh	*Sunflowers*

Sources for art prints

Modern Learning Press
POB 167, Dept 32
Rosemont, NJ 08556

Museum of Fine Arts
POB 1044
Boston, MA 02120

University Prints
Box 485
Winchester, MA 01890

Decor Prints
Box 502
Noel, MO 64854

Use the following picture books as a comparison to particular artists:

Artist	Book
Matisse	*On the Day You Were Born* by Debora Frasier
Rembrandt	*Rembrandt's Beret* by Johnny Alcorn
Monet	*Linnea in Monet's Garden* by Christina Bjork
Chagall	*Pythons' Party* by Brian Wildsmith
Klee	*Stay Up Late* by Maria Kalmans

Part II

Focusing:
From Book to Art

This section takes particular works of children's literature and pairs each with a particular creative idea. Each activity includes a focus book, a synopsis, an "ARTivity," and additional books and references. An Artivity is an art experience that can be directly related to the theme of the Focus Book. Each Artivity has items for discussion or thought, a materials list, directions and suggestions.

1

FOCUS BOOK

Fish Eyes:
A Book You Can Count On.
Lois Ehlert.
Harcourt Brace Jovanovich,
1990.

This is a colorful counting book that shows many different fish that a child might see if he/she became a fish too. Beautifully colored and patterned geometric fish appear throughout.

ARTivity: Felty Fish

Make a fish tank that does not have the problems of feeding and cleaning! Fill it with funny felt fish. This group activity helps build social skills, fine motor skills, and creativity. This book is appropriate to motivate children to be interested in the beauty of exotic fish. After sharing the book *Fish Eyes,* talk about fish and what they look like. Ask the children:

- What kinds of body shapes do fish have?
- Can you name some parts of a fish body?
- What other creatures live underwater?
- What do fish eat?
- What kinds of patterns and colors do fish have?
- If you made your own fish, what would it look like?

The children are ready to design their fish. They will complete the creative process by first making a paper pattern of their idea, and then making a three-dimensional art work.

Materials needed (for each child)

One 8″ × 8″ square of felt of a chosen color
Scissors
Paper
Pencil
Cotton balls for stuffing
Needle and thread or sewing machine
Glue
Sequins, scrap material
Pins

Have the children draw an outline of the shape of their imagined fish, including fins and tail, on the paper. Next, they cut out the shape to make a pattern. Pin the pattern to the felt and trace around it with a pencil. Be sure to make two

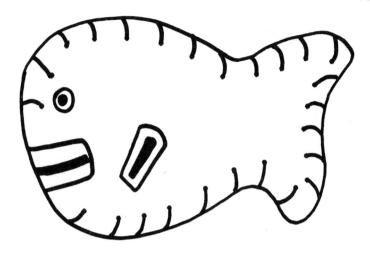

fish shapes. Cut out the shapes. Pin the pieces together and stuff with cotton balls. Children can then sew or glue the shapes together. If you have a sewing machine or a volunteer who has one, the fish can be sewn on the machine. Now the children can decorate their fish with sequins, scraps, and any other materials available.

A box can be used to create an aquarium. Simply cut a square out of the side. Decorate with paper or plastic plants and sea shells. Fish can be hung from the top using heavy thread. Another way to display the fish is to hang a sheet of butcher paper on a wall and let the children decorate it like an underwater scene. Felt fish are light enough to be attached to the paper scene with tape.

Related Books and References

Arnosky, Jim. *Fish in a Flash*. Bradbury, 1991.

Elborn, Andrew. *Big Al*. Picture Book Studio, 1988.

Evans, Mark. *Fish: A Practical Guide for Caring for Your Fish*. (ASPCA Pet Care Guides for Kids) Dorling Kindersley, 1993.

Filisky, Michael. *Fishes*. (Peterson First Guides) Houghton Mifflin, 1989.

Lavies, Bianca. *The Atlantic Salmon*. Dutton, 1992.

MacCarty, Patricia. *Ocean Parade: A Counting Book*. Dial, 1990.

Pallotta, Jerry. *The Underwater Alphabet Book*. Charlesbridge Publishing, 1991.

Sussman, Susan. *Big Friend, Little Friend: A Book About Symbiosis*. Houghton Mifflin, 1989.

2

FOCUS BOOK

Totem Pole.
Diane Hoyt Goldsmith.
Holiday House, 1990.

A Tsimshian Indian boy describes how his father designs and carves a totem pole for the Klallam tribe in Washington state. Beautiful color photographs show Native American artifacts and ways. Write to the artist of the totem pole, David Boxley, at POB 527, Kingston, WA 98346.

ARTivity: Tribe Totem

This is a cooperative activity for a group. The interaction between the children promotes socialization. The creative process is enhanced by the fact that everyone contributes to the project in some way. The project also exercises visual discrimination and design skills. Talk about the fact that totem poles are made in many different Native American cultures. Show the book *Totem Pole,* which has photos of a totem from the Klallam Tribe of Washington State. Brainstorm together the types of animals or figures the children would like to have on their totem. The use of "authentic" Native American figures is not as important as hearing all ideas. Make a list of the characteristics, colors, animals, and figures decided upon.

Materials needed

Newspaper
Glue
Various cardboard boxes
Old paintbrush
Scissors
Crayons, markers, or paint and brushes

Have the children each draw a sketch of the totem as they see it, using the elements the group has chosen. Decide which design to use. Display all other designs on a bulletin board. Tape the chosen design up for all to see. Count the number of sections in the design and set out the right number of boxes. Assign groups to decorate each section using the design as a general guide. Assign one group to use cardboard to make an animal or figure for the top of the pole. Spread newspapers on the floor and have the children decorate each section using crayons, markers, or paint. Build up the totem by gluing the individual boxes on top of each other, allowing the glue to dry before the next box is added. Glue the fig-

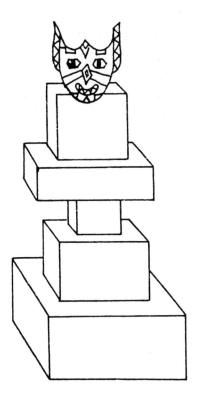

ure for the top of the pole on last. A totem pole such as this can serve as an interesting centerpiece for drama, dance, or a unit of study on Native American art.

Related Books and References

Ancona, George. *Powwow*. Harcourt Brace Jovanovich, 1993.

Batdorf, Carol. *Totem Poles: An Ancient Art*. Hancock House, 1990.

Bernstein, Bonnie. *Native American Crafts Workshop.* Fearon Teacher Aides, 1982.

Siberell, Anne. *Whale in the Sky.* Dutton, 1985.

Yue, David and Charlotte. *The Tipi: A Center of Native American Life.* Knopf, 1984.

3

FOCUS BOOK

Large as Life Nighttime Animals. Joanna Cole. Alfred A. Knopf, 1985.

This book has beautifully illustrated watercolor paintings of small nocturnal creatures in full size. Included are elf owl, fennec fox, chinchilla, royal antelope, and giant toad.

ARTivity: Animal "Giants"

Three-dimensional animal "sculptures" can be made from simple materials. This art project helps children with planning skills, anatomy, and realistic drawing. Share the book *Large as Life Nighttime Animals.* Discuss the concept of sizes with the children. Let them tell you which animal from the book is their favorite and why. Record their answers on poster or chalkboard. Each child will now choose an animal to make, either from the book or any other creature. Have the children go to the library and research their animals to get the right dimensions and coloring. Emphasize that the representations they make are to be realistic and life size.

Materials needed (for each child)

Kraft paper or paper sacks
Chalk
Newspapers
Tempera paint and brushes
Scissors
Yarn
Shellac
Large-eyed needles or hole punches
Scrap materials for decorations

Have the children measure out the right amount of kraft paper to make their animals. Spread newspaper on the work space. Each child draws an animal on the paper with chalk. Have them draw details also. Mistakes can be erased with a chalkboard eraser. The "Giant Animals" are then cut out, being careful to cut both pieces to form a front and back. Next, paint both the front and rear views of the animals. If a coat of shellac is painted over the tempera, it will last longer and not crack. After the animals dry, sew them together using the needles and yarn. An alternative method is to punch holes around the edge of both pieces of kraft paper. The pieces can then be "sewn" with yarn. A good sized opening must be left

so that wads of newspaper stuffing can be placed inside. After stuffing, sew the hole closed. Any scrap materials that are needed to complete the animals can now be added.

Related Books or References

Ball, Jacqueline. *What Can It Be?* Silver Press, 1989.

Crump, Donald J. *Creatures Small and Furry*. National Geographic Society, 1983.

Hirschi, Ron. *A Time for Babies*. Cobblehill, 1993.

Kitchen, Bert. *And So They Build*. Candlewick Press, 1993.

————. *Somewhere Today*. Candlewick Press, 1993.

Lilly, Kenneth. *Kenneth Lilly's Animals: A Portfolio of Paintings*. Lothrop, Lee & Shepard, 1988.

Machotla, Hana. *What Neat Feet!* Morrow, 1991.

Powzyk, Joyce. *Tasmania: A Wildlife Journey*. Lothrop, 1987.

Sierra Club Book of Small Mammals. Weldon Owen, 1993.

Yamashita, Keiko. *Paws, Wings, and Hooves: Animals on the Move*. Lerner, 1993.

4

FOCUS BOOK

Monarch Butterflies: Mysterious Travelers. Bianca Lavies. Dutton, 1992.

This beautifully photographed book describes the life and habits of the monarch butterfly. Stunning close-ups and charming photos of landed monarchs make this especially good for sharing.

ARTivity: Stained Glass Butterflies

Discuss the metamorphosis of butterflies and moths. Ask the children what a butterfly would look like if they designed it. The following activity introduces the medium of crayons as well as color mixing.

Materials needed (For each child)

Black construction paper
Old crayons
2 8½″ × 11″ pieces of wax paper
Plastic knife
Scissors
Glue
Pipe cleaner
Iron
Old towel
Hole punch

It is preferable that children draw their own outline of a butterfly like a stained glass outline. Cut out the pattern twice. Take the plastic knife and shave bits of crayon onto the wax paper. Tell the children to use many colors, but leave some clear spaces. Cover the shavings with another wax paper. Place the old towel over the wax paper and iron the papers together so that the shavings melt. Point out to the children how colors that overlapped have melted together to form new colors. Glue one butterfly cutout to the now colored wax paper. Trim the excess wax paper from around the outside of the butterfly. Match up the second butterfly cutout and glue it to the other side so that the wax paper is sandwiched between. Punch a hole where the head is and twist a pipe cleaner through it. The butterflies are attractive when displayed on a window where the light can shine through. The children can also arrange their creations in a group pattern to make a large "stained glass" design.

Related Books or Resources

Charles, Oz. *How Is a Crayon Made?* Simon and Schuster, 1988.

Deluise, Dom. *Charlie the Caterpillar*. Simon and Schuster, 1990.

Feltwell, John. *Butterflies and Moths*. Dorling Kindersley, 1993.

French, Vivian. *Caterpillar, Caterpillar*. Candlewick Press, 1993.

Grifalconi, Anne. *Darkness and the Butterfly*. Little Brown, 1987.

Pluckrose, Henry. *Crayons*. Franklin Watts, 1987.

Quiri, Patricia R. *Metamorphosis*. Franklin Watts, 1991.

Ryder, Joanne. *Where Butterflies Grow*. Dutton, 1989.

5

FOCUS BOOK

The Emperor and the Kite.
Jane Yolen. Philomel, 1988.

In ancient China the smallest daughter of an emperor is ignored by her family. This princess, Dejow Seow, passes her time making kites. When her father is imprisoned in a tall tower, she cleverly uses her kite to rescue him.

Kites are an exciting, satisfying art form that can lead directly to studies in science (wind and air), math (measuring and dimensions), and history (kites in different cultures).

ARTivity: Chinese Fish Kite

Flying kites has been popular in Asia since 1000 B.C. Kites held great religious significance and were believed to keep away evil spirits when flown at night. September 9 is "Kite Day" in China.

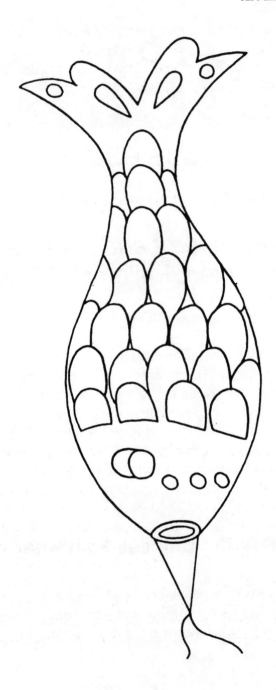

Since the story *The Emperor and the Kite* is set in China, here is a Chinese design to make. The results of this activity make a beautiful display when suspended from the ceiling. These models are rather fragile and are not recommended for actual flying. For designs that really fly, see the book *Kites on the Wind: Easy to Make Kites that Fly Without Sticks.*

Materials needed (For each child)

Tissue paper
Pencil
Scissors
Wire
Wire cutters
String
Glue
Old paint brush

Have the children place two sheets of tissue paper of a chosen color on top of each other on a flat surface. Next, they draw an outline of a fish on the top sheet, using as much of the tissue paper as possible. The next step is to cut out the shape through both layers of tissue. Children can now glue the two shapes together around the outer edges, leaving the mouth area open. Let the glue dry. An adult may need to bend sections of wire into circles to fit the fishes' mouths. Children can tie two 12″ lengths of string to the wire circle opposite each other. An adult may need to help each child carefully insert the wire circle into the fishes' mouths and fold a small edge over to cover the wire. Secure this edge with glue and let it dry. Decorate the fish with scrap tissue or

crayons. Tie the lengths of string together. The kites are ready
to be displayed.

Related Books or References

Evans, David. *Fishing for Angels: The Magic of Kites*. Annick Press, 1991.

Gibbons, Gail. *Catch the Wind*. Little Brown, 1989.

Kelly, Emery J. *Kites on the Wind: Easy to Make Kites that
   Fly Without Sticks*. Lerner, 1991.

Lies, Brian. *Hamlet and the Enormous Chinese Dragon
   Kite*. Houghton Mifflin, 1994.

MacDonald, Maryann. *Rabbit's Birthday Kite*. Bantam,
   1991.

Morgan, Paul and Helene. *The Ultimate Kite Book*. Simon
   and Schuster, 1992.

Reddix, Valerie. *Dragon Kite of the Autumn Moon*. Lothrop,
   1991.

6

FOCUS BOOK

Vejigante Masquerader. Lulu Delacre. Scholastic, 1993.

Ramon is a Puerto Rican boy who wants to be a vejigante, or costumed masquerader, for Carnival in his country. To do so, he must secretly make his own costume and vejigante mask. Unfortunately, Ramon gets in a bind when an unfriendly goat rips his costume.

ARTivity: Masks

Masks have been used for celebrations and rituals throughout history. An example from one culture is depicted in the story *Vejigante Masquerader*. Today we occasionally use masks for Mardi Gras or Halloween. Mask making is also an art form in itself. The following activity incorporates color theory and line design skills. Discuss the concept of design as a

plan for the artwork with the children. Tell them they will combine shapes, patterns, and lines to form an interesting mask.

Materials needed (for each child)

Paper
Pencil
Paper plate
Black permanent waterproof marker
Tempera paint, pastels, or crayon—three colors in either
    warm (orange, yellow, red), cool (blue, purple, green), or
    primary (red, yellow, blue) tones.
Brushes (if paint is used)

Have each child draw several different ideas for a mask. Tell them to use lines, shapes and patterns, such as those on the vejigante masks. Their designs can be animals, people, or imaginary characters. Next, the children can select their favorite design. This should be carefully drawn in pencil on the *bottom* of the paper plate. The pencil lines can then be drawn over with the permanent marker. The next step is to choose a color scheme and color or paint the design with a heavy coating of color. The resulting masks are colorful and worth keeping.

Related Books or Resources

Alkema, Jay. *Masks*. Sterling, 1971.

Baylor, Byrd. *They Put on Masks*. Scribner, 1974.

Couvillon, Alice and Elizabeth Moore. *Mimi's First Mardi Gras*. Pelican, 1992.

Green, Jen. *Making Crazy Faces and Masks*. Gloucester, 1992.

Pitcher, Caroline (consultant). *Masks and Puppets*. Franklin Watts, 1984.

Robson, Denny. *Masks and Funny Faces*. Gloucester, 1991.

7

FOCUS BOOK

Spiders.
Donna Bailey.
Heinemann, 1991.

An easy to read and understand factual book about spiders. This book explains a spider's body parts, web, habits, and life cycle. Interesting close-up color photographs are found throughout.

ARTivity: Spider Webs

There are many wonderful artistic designs, patterns, and forms in nature. Use the book *Spider's Web* to explain just how one particular natural "art work" is done. Compare the facts and fictions about spiders, reading aloud from *Someone Saw a Spider*.

Design and pattern are emphasized in this simple project.

Materials needed (for each child)

Black construction paper
Glue and small glue bottles
Yellow powdered tempera paint

An adult will mix the powdered tempera with the glue to give it color. Put the glue in small glue bottles, one for each child. Let the children experiment, designing different patterns of spider webs by applying lines of glue to construction paper. Allow the webs to dry completely. When dry, the raised web designs will be similar to those created by Eric Carle in *The Very Busy Spider*.

Related Books or Resources

Back, Christine and Barrie Watts. *Spider's Web*. Silver Burdett, 1984.

Berger, Melvin. *Stranger Than Fiction*. Avon, 1990.

Carle, Eric. *The Very Busy Spider*. Philomel, 1985.

Climo, Shirley. *Someone Saw a Spider: Spider Facts and Folktales*. Thomas Y. Crowell, 1985.

Kajpust, Melissa. *A Dozen Silk Diapers*. Hyperion, 1993.

Kimmel, Eric. *Anansi Goes Fishing*. Holiday House, 1992.

Kirk, David. *Miss Spider's Tea Party*. Scholastic, 1994.

MacDonald, Suse. *Space Spinners*. Dial, 1991.

Schnieper, Claudia. *Amazing Spiders*. Carolrhoda Books, 1989.

8

FOCUS BOOK

The Trouble with Dad.
Babette Cole. Putnam, 1986.

Dad's fantastic robot creations cause a family to have incredible adventures.

ARTivity: Robot City

Using photograms, create a village for robots. Discuss with the children what they would like a robot to do for them, as well as what it might look like. Also, decide what kinds of machines and vehicles would be in a robot village. Have the children gather up discarded jewelry, tool parts, kitchen utensils, keys, and other small found objects. Robots are designed by laying the objects in a pattern on a sheet of blueprint paper.

For each child, you will need paper towels, found objects, cardboard squares, scissors, old newspaper, and a piece of blueprint paper cut from a roll. (Blueprint paper can be purchased or donated from a duplicating or blueprint company.) You will also need two plastic dishpans, a table near a window, and 3% hydrogen peroxide (available at the drugstore).

Mix ½ cup peroxide with a gallon of water in one of the dishpans. Fill the other tray with cool water. Spread newspapers over the surface of the table. Have the children recompose their robots on the blueprint paper, which is placed on a cardboard square. Do the composing away from the window with the blue side of the paper up. Each child carries his/her design to the table by the window and leaves it in bright sun for one to two minutes. If the day is overcast, exposure will take longer. After exposure, remove the found objects from the paper. Immerse the blueprint paper in the hydrogen peroxide water for a few seconds.

The background of the paper will turn bright blue, while the robot image silhouette will turn white. Rinse the photogram in the clear water for a few seconds and blot dry with a paper towel. Lay the prints flat on the table to dry. If desired, designs can be glued to cardboard and stood up with triangular stands or put on a bulletin board.

Related Books and Resources

Barrett, N.S. *Robots*. Franklin Watts, 1985.

Dupasquire, Phillipe. *A Robot Named Chip*. Viking, 1991.

Lauber, Patricia. *Get Ready for Robots*. Thomas Y. Crowell, 1987.

Montgomery, R.A. *Your Very Own Robot*. Bantam, 1982.

Petty, Kate. *Robots*. Franklin Watts, 1987.

9

FOCUS BOOK

Linnea's Almanac.
Christina Bjork.
R&S Books, 1989.

Linnea, a young girl, keeps track of all the activities she does around the year. This includes all kinds of nature tidbits, ideas, and activities; charming illustrations, and instructions for organizing collections, such as leaves, beach treasures, and mementos.

ARTivity: Collections

Children can learn a lot from making collections. An early collection could lead to a hobby later in life. Arranging and displaying collections provides useful opportunities for sorting and classifying. Collections reveal the language, habits, and interests of the collector, as well as the heritage of past generations. A collection is an accumulation of related objects or specimens consciously chosen for unity. Art history and appreciation can be taught with collections.

Kids can also collect: stickers, wrappers, leaves, bottle-tops, postcards, feathers, tickets, and more. Have children assemble their own collections as part of arranging and displaying activities. Limit collections to low-cost or free items. No matter what is collected, the children will experience research, acquisition, and classification. Display and discuss the work of Joseph Cornell, Louise Nevelson, and Richard Stankiewicz, who do collection collages and assemblages. Have the children then create their own collection collages.

Techniques of collecting and preservation in a museum can also be introduced through collections. Provide information on museumology and historical methods of investigation. Explain that collections in museums are made up of artifacts, which are objects made by people that can reveal information about a particular culture and the environment. Artifacts help historians piece together the past. Artifacts can be tools, clothing, toys, jewelry, or weapons.

Divide the children into three groups and give each group the following: Group one—clay, sponges, and cardboard; Group two—feathers, yarn, beads, and straws; Group three—ribbons, sticks, berries, and bark. Have each group design an artifact using their materials. All three groups should answer the following questions about their artifact:

1. What is the artifact used for?
2. How is it used?
3. How would this artifact be classified? (Tool, jewelry, toy, weapon, etc.)

Additional Resources and References

Anderson, Lena. *Stina*. Greenwillow, 1989.

Bonners, Susan. *The Wooden Doll*. Lothrop, Lee & Shepard, 1991.

Engel, Diana. *Josephina, the Great Collector*. Morrow, 1988.

Greenblatt, Rodney. *Aunt Ippy's Museum of Junk*. Harper Collins, 1991.

Johnson, Pamela. *A Mouse's Tale*. Harcourt, 1991.

Ockenga, Starr. *The Ark in the Attic*. David R. Godine, 1987.

Price-Thomas, Brian. *The Magic Ark*. Crown, 1987.

Tofts, Hanna. *The Collage Book*. Simon and Schuster, 1991.

Westell, Kerry. *Amanda's Book*. Firefly, 1991.

Part III

Exploring: From Art to Book

Part Three allows us to take a visual art method and explore it fully through examples from both children's literature and from art history. Each art method includes books to show as examples, books about the particular method, and books about artists who work in that medium or method. Also included are objectives for the activity, vocabulary words, brief related information, how to relate the artistic method to other curricular areas through simple activities, and a culminating activity that uses the particular artistic medium or method.

1

Painting

Examples of painting in picture books

Baker, Keith. *Hide and Snake*. Harcourt, Brace, Jovanovich, 1991. (acrylic)

Brown, Ken. *Why Can't I Fly?* Doubleday, 1990. (watercolor)

Fisher, Leonard Everett. *Boxes! Boxes!* Viking, 1984. (acrylic)

Florian, Douglas. *A Painter*. Greenwillow, 1993. (watercolor)

George, William T. *Fishing at Long Pond*. Greenwillow, 1991. [Pictures by Lindsay B. George.] (gouache)

Greenfield, Eloise. *First Pink Light*. Writers and Readers Publications, 1991. (gouache and pastel)

Johnston, Tony. *Yonder*. Dial, 1988. [Pictures by Lloyd Bloom.] (oil)

Kasza, Keiko. *The Wolf's Chicken Stew*. Putnam, 1987. (watercolor)

Smith, Lane. *Glasses: Who Needs 'Em?* Viking, 1991. (oil)

Stanley, Diane. *The Gentleman and the Kitchen Maid*. Dial, 1994. [Pictures by Dennis Nolan.] (oil)

Books about how to paint

Muller, Brunhild. *Painting with Children*. Edinburgh, Scotland: Floris Books, 1987.

Pekarick, Andrew. *Painting*. California: Walt Disney Books, 1992.

Pluckrose, Henry. *Paints*. New York: Watts, 1988.

Solga, Kim. *Paint!* New York: North Light Books, 1991.

Artists to study

Everett, Gwen. *Lil Sis and Uncle Willie: The Life and Paintings of William H. Johnson*. Washington, DC: Smithsonian, 1991.

Muhlberger, Richard. *What Makes a Dégas a Dégas?* Viking, 1993.

Sills, Leslie. *Visions: Stories About Women Artists*. Albert Whitman, 1993.

Skira-Venturi, Rosabianca. *A Weekend with Dégas*. New York: Rizzoli, 1991.

Venezia, Mike. *Van Gogh.* Chicago: Children's Press, 1988.

Walker, Lou Ann. *Roy Lichtenstein: Artist at Work.* Lodestar, 1994.

Zhensun, Sheng, and Alice Low. *A Young Painter: The Life and Paintings of Wang Yani.* New York: Scholastic, 1991.

Objectives

1. Recognize paintings as works of art.
2. Learn different painting mediums and methods.
3. Discover some painters and their work.

Related Vocabulary

Oil, acrylic, watercolor, gouache, landscape, portrait, abstract, still life, canvas, palette.

Painting is probably the kind of visual art that is most familiar to children. To become a good painter, one must paint. It is important to get a feel for the paint, rather than worry about the finished product. Obtain as many different types of paint as you can and let the children experiment and spend time understanding how each one looks on the page.

Reading and Language Arts

Share the poem "The Starry Night," by Anne Sexton, from *All My Pretty Ones* (Houghton Mifflin, 1961), p.9. Show the painting by Vincent Van Gogh, "Starry Night."

Choose an artist from the list of suggested prints in Part One. Let the children view the print and write a short poem about their feelings or responses to the print.

Social Studies

Travel: Choose several historically significant painters from all over the world. Assign a group a particular painter. Have each group design a travel brochure about that country. Tell them to include facts about industry, population, culture, as well as information about the artist.

Math

Pointillism: Introduce Georges Seurat's late-19th-century style using dots to make images. Trace or copy outlines of simple objects and let the children fill in the outlines with tiny dots from felt tip pens. Tell them to count the dots as they make them.

Dot Box: Using paper and a pencil, illustrate 25 dots evenly spaced in five columns of five. Play a geometry game, seeing who can form the most triangles using the dots in the arrangement.

Fractions: Find a reproduction of the any of the "Watermelon" paintings by Rufino Tamayo. Purchase a real watermelon and discuss fractions by cutting the melon in 1/2, 1/3, 1/4, etc. Have the children paint the different fractions of watermelon.

Science

Color Bags: Measure and mix the following in a zip-lock bag: 1/3 cup sugar, 1 cup cold water starch, food coloring of two chosen colors, and two cups water. You now have color mixing in a bag. Make up several bags of two colors and have the children squeeze and squash the bags to mix them.

Music and Drama

Picture Plays: Find several art prints of paintings that are still life. Recreate with real objects the composition and colors in the painting as closely as possible. Talk about the balance and harmony of the still life. Have the group use the still life as a starting place for a short play or dramatic scene.

Culminating Activity: Adopt a Masterpiece

Help children appreciate the particular style and work in a painting. Obtain prints of paintings that have child appeal,

one for each participant. Have each child select a print to
"adopt." The print becomes the painting on which he/she will
focus, gathering biographical information about the artist,
the style and time period, the mood, color, and shapes. Each

child also takes the print home and hangs it in a prominent place to spark discussion with his/her family.

Introduce an "Artist of the Week," helping students to identify the colors, themes, and methods of particular artists. Have a "We're Painters" day. Each child makes a copy or a tracing of a print to color. They will change colors, add or delete objects. Finally, the children relate what they have discovered about their paintings on "Be the Art" day. Have them come in costumes related to the subject of the paintings or make a "body mask" of the painting to wear. (A body mask is a child's recreation of the work with a hole cut out for the child's face to appear in the art.)

2

Color

Examples of color in picture books

Allington, Richard. *Beginning to Learn About Colors*. Raintree, 1979.

Felix, Monique. *The Colors*. Creative Education, 1991.

Fisher, Leonard Everett. *Storm at the Jetty*. Viking, 1981. (tones of gray with black and white)

Jonas, Ann. *Color Dance*. Greenwillow, 1989. (color mixing)

Konigsburg, E.L. *Samuel Todd's Book of Great Colors*. Atheneum, 1990.

My Little Color Book series. Photos by Jerry Young. Dorling Kindersley, 1993.

Oliver, Stephen. *My First Look at Colors*. Random House, 1990.

Silshe, Brenda. *Just One More Color*. Annick Press, 1991.

Watson, Carol, and Heather Amery. *Colors*. Usborne, 1984.

Books about color

Anderson, L.W. *Light and Color*. Raintree, 1978.

Johnston, Tom. *Light! Color! Action!* Gareth Stevens, 1988

Kirkpatrick, Rena A. *Look at Rainbow Colors*. Raintree, 1978.

Westray, Kathleen. *A Color Sampler*. Ticknor and Fields, 1993.

Yenawine, Philip. *Colors*. Delacorte, 1991.

Artists to study

Ball, Jacqueline A. and Catherine Conant. *Georgia O'Keeffe*. Blackbirch Press, 1991.

Frazier, Nancy. *Frida Kahlo*. Blackbirch, 1992.

Grazel, Sue, and Kathy Halbreich. *Elizabeth Murray: Paintings and Drawings*. Harry N. Abrams, 1987.

Turner, Robyn M. *Rosa Bonheur*. Little Brown, 1991.

Objectives

1. To learn the basic color principles of warm, cool, absorption, and reflection.
2. To practice mixing colors.
3. To understand the color wheel and complementary or contrasting color.

Related vocabulary

Complementary color, contrasting color, tint, shade, reflection, absorption, spectrum.

Color surrounds us in our daily lives. All things, natural or man-made, contain color. We each think and respond differently to color. Color is also found in all types of art. Children respond especially well to color. Ask them questions about how they feel and about their favorite colors. Colors are warm or cool. Warm colors are reds, oranges, and yellows, like the sun and fall leaves. Cool colors are blues, greens, and purples, such as water or the forest. Warm colors look closer in a picture, while cool colors seem farther away. Colors can also evoke emotion. Think of some of the common expressions the children might have heard, such as "seeing red," "feeling blue," or "green with envy." Colors can also be warm (red/yellow shades) or cool (blue/green shades). White is the reflection of all colors, and black is the absorption of all colors.

Reading and Language Arts

Share the picture book *Color: A Poem* by Christina Rossetti. Point out the pattern of each verse, such as:
    What is blue?
    The sky is blue
    When the day is new.

Have the children follow the pattern of the verses with their own ideas about color:

First line: What is _____? (Color)
Second line: A _____ (Object) is _____. (Color)
Third line: (Add a line that rhymes with the color)

Remind the children of the words that bring particular colors to mind, such as sad, hot, winter, loud, Christmas, night, and autumn. These can be used in their verses. Show examples of unusual colors, such as ebony, scarlet, turquoise, mauve, magenta, coral, and ivory. Encourage use of these colors also. Have the children learn and recite their poems.

Social Studies

Quick color games: Send the kids on a color scavenger hunt, where they gather up objects from a list of colors. Or, have them write a color description of an object using as many colors as possible.

Color Symbolism: Colors have been used historically as symbols in many different cultures. For example, some traditional color symbols are:

   Purple—Royalty
   Red—Blood
   Black—Grief

Color symbols are also used today. Red, white, and blue stand for America; red means stop at a stop sign, while green means go; red and green together remind us of Christmas.

Color Picnic: You will need a picnic basket, scissors, and various colored sheets of construction paper. Tell the children you are going on a Color Picnic. Have each child cut various shapes of food from different colors, then pile them into the basket. When the basket is ready, sit down on the floor and pass out the shapes. Using the colors as a clue, the children name a food of that shape and color.

Math

Measure and Chart: Use the color mixing bag activity in the science section on painting. Measure each ingredient. Make a chart or graph of the color results obtained.

Match Matches: To develop number/numeral correspondence, make two sets of 4″ × 6″ cards. Each set has pairs with colored dots on one and the corresponding number on the other. Match by numerals and then sort by color.

Science

Absorption: Take 1″ pieces of colored tissue paper and place them in a pattern on a sheet of white paper. Overlap some colors. Spray with water from a plastic spray bottle. After the tissues dry, lift them off and discard. The white paper will have absorbed the color from the tissue. Discuss absorption and reflection.

On a warm day, the sun's heat will be absorbed by different colors. Place sheets of various colored construction paper in direct sunlight. Be sure to include black and white. Next place one ice cube in several plastic bags and seal.

Place the bags on each sheet of paper. Observe which cubes melt first. A thermometer can also be placed on each sheet for 15 minutes. The hottest color has absorbed the most heat.

Colorful Animals: Study chameleons and other animals that can change their colors to camouflage themselves. Another interesting science activity is to make a display of the color of feathers, identifying birds and their coloration.

Music and Drama

Color Dance: Use the book *Color Dance* by Ann Jonas (Greenwillow, 1989). Obtain sheer scarves or fabric, as used in the pictures. Have the children dance and combine the scarves to make the colors as done in the book.

Song: Sing "The Color Clothes Song" (To the tune of "Mary Had a Little Lamb")

> Blue, blue, blue, blue,
> Who is wearing blue today?
> Blue, blue, blue, blue,
> Who is wearing blue today?
>
> I am wearing blue today,
> blue today, blue today
> Look at me and you will say,
> I am wearing blue today.

(Repeat with various colors)

Culminating Activity

Discover Colors: For each child you will need a 5″ × 6″ sheet of white paper, one tablespoon of black powdered tempera paint, old newspapers to protect your work surface, three tablespoons of liquid detergent, crayons, a plastic cup, a paintbrush, and a scraper tool (a metal nail file or nail will do fine).

Put the powdered paint into the cup and add detergent. Mix until the paint is thick and creamy (add more paint if needed). Color the paper heavily with various colored crayons. Make patterns and overlap colors. Brush the paint mixture on to the paper. The paint should cover the entire paper. Let it dry. Decide on a design, and scrape it into the surface of the paint with the scraper tool. Be careful not to press too hard and tear the paper. As the paint is removed, the colors of the crayon will show through in the lines of the design.

3

Drawing

Examples of drawing in picture books

Ackerman, Karen. *Song and Dance Man.* [Pictures by Stephen Gammell] Knopf, 1988. (colored pencil)

Adoff, Arnold. *In for Winter, Out for Spring.* [Pictures by Jerry Pinkney] Harcourt, Brace, Jovanovich, 1991. (pencil, colored pencil, pastel)

Alexander, Lloyd. *The Fortune Tellers.* [Pictures by Trina Schart Hyman] Dutton, 1992. (ink, crayon, and acrylic)

Armstrong, Jennifer. *Chin Yu Min and the Ginger Cat.* [Pictures by Mary Grandpré] Crown, 1993. (pastel)

Arnosky, Jim. *Raccoons and Ripe Corn.* Lothrop, Lee and Shepard, 1987. (Pencil and watercolor)

Carlstrom, Nancy White. *Goodbye Geese.* [Pictures by Ed Young] Philomel, 1991. (pastel)

Carlstrom, Nancy White. *Where Does the Night Hide?* [Pictures by Thomas Allan] Macmillan, 1990.

Potter, Katherine. *Spike*. Simon and Schuster, 1994.

Van Allsburg, Chris. *Jumanji*. Houghton Mifflin, 1981. (Conté crayon)

Books about drawing

Arnosky, Jim. *Drawing Life in Motion*. Lothrop, Lee and Shepard, 1984.

Martin, Judy. *Painting and Drawing*. Milbrook, 1994.

Pluckrose, Henry. *Crayons*. Franklin Watts, 1987.

Vaughn-Jackson, Gene. *Sketching and Drawing for Children*. Perigee, 1990.

Witty, Ken. *A Day in the Life of an Illustrator*. Troll, 1981.

Artists to study

Collins, David R. *The Country Artist: A Story About Beatrix Potter*. Carolrhoda, 1989.

Italia, Robert. *Mickey Mouse*. Abdo and Daughters, 1991. (Walt Disney)

Kurtzmann, Harvey. *My Life as an Artist*. Minstrel Books, 1988.

Reef, Pat. *Dahlov Ipcar, Artist*. Kennebec River, 1987.

Objectives

1. To discover different drawing media such as pens, pencils, pen and ink, pastel, charcoal.
2. To understand different kinds of lines, masses, and shadows formed by drawing.

Related Vocabulary

Charcoal, pastel, ebony, pastel, media, line, mass, shadow.

Kids like to draw and most are very experienced at it. Drawing is the pre-writing stage, and baby babbling is the pre-speaking stage. Explore, contrast and compare the drawing tools and the results shown in the various books listed.

Reading and Language Arts

Pictures Tell a Story: Choose several prints of drawings. Artists to use are Beatrix Potter, Walt Disney, etc. Display them and let each child choose drawings that appeal. Have them write a one-page story about the people, circumstances, or meaning of the drawing.

Art Adjective: Have each child choose an adjective and draw the word in a way that reflects the definition. For example, skinny might be drawn in tall stick letters, while fat could be drawn in short, thick letters.

Social Studies

Beatrix Potter: Share the book *Country Artist*. This book makes a good springboard to study the culture and time period of Potter.

Me Books: The children can make tiny picture books like Potter's. Tell them to draw self-portraits and other family members. Stories can also be written about each person in their books.

Math

Counting Book: You will need oaktag, crayons, a hole punch, metal rings, scissors. Cut the oaktag into five-by-five squares and give each child ten of them. Punch a hole in each square in the upper left corner and put on a metal ring. Have the children put one number on each card, from 1 to 10. Now they will draw objects to represent each number.

Design a Dollar: Using pencils and paper, have each child design his/her own dollar bill, using lots of fine lines. Discuss the different ways to make change for a dollar—20 nickels; 50 pennies and two quarters; seven dimes, one quarter, five pennies. There are 300 ways to make change for a dollar!

Science

Fire Drawing: Fire can be studied for its effects on man and the environment. Fire affects the soil, air, plants, water, and animal life. Charcoal is the drawing material that can be produced by fire. Using found charcoal from an old burnt tree or a barbecue, the children can explore this drawing medium.

Music and Drama

Dance Draw: Music can inspire drawing. With drawing supplies and paper ready, choose different styles and types of music to play—fast, slow, classical, rock, ethnic. Have the children think about the colors, shapes and images the music brings to mind. Have them transfer their ideas to paper. Next play Moussorgsky's "Pictures at an Exhibition." Play movements and let the children try to guess the auditory picture being "drawn" by the sounds. Movements of the piece to use are "Gnome," "Landscape," "Children," "Chicks," "Ox Cart," and "Market."

Culminating Activity

Cinnamon Drawing: This activity is pleasing to both the eye and the nose! You will need cinnamon sticks, fine-grade sandpaper, and scissors. The children simply draw on the sandpaper using the cinnamon stick as a tool. The pictures can be mounted, or cut out and hung as sachets.

4

Printmaking

Examples of printmaking in picture books

Albert, Burton. *Where Does the Trail Lead?* [Pictures by Brian Pinkney] Simon and Schuster, 1991. (Scratch board renderings)

D'Aulaire, Ingri, and Edgar Parin. *Abraham Lincoln.* Dell, 1939. (Lithograph)

Day, Edward C. *John Tabor's Ride.* [Pictures by Dirk Zimmer] Knopf, 1989. (Etching)

De Armond, Dale. *The Seal Oil Lamp.* Sierra Club Books, 1988. (Wood engravings)

Jaffe, Nina. *In the Month of Kislev.* [Pictures by Louise August] Viking, 1992. (Woodcut)

Knutson, Barbara. *Why the Crab Has No Head.* Carolrhoda, 1987. (Linocut)

Tejima, Keizaburo. *Fox's Dream.* Philomel, 1985. (Japanese woodcut)

Xiong, Blia. *Nine-In-One Grr! Grr!* [Pictures by Nancy Hom] Children's Book Press, 1989. (Silkscreen)

Books about printmaking

Fleischman, Paul. *Copier Creations*. Harper Collins, 1993.

Hart, Tony. *Printing and Patterns*. Windmill Press, 1983.

Rockwell, Harlow. *Printmaking*. Doubleday, 1973.

Tofts, Hannah. *The Print Book*. Simon and Schuster, 1989.

Artists to study

Bockris, Victor. *The Life and Death of Andy Warhol*. Bantam, 1990.

Objectives

1. Learn how to plan a design and translate it to another medium.
2. Learn basic printmaking techniques.
3. Discover the idea of multiple images.

Related Vocabulary

Etching, lithograph, monoprint, serigraph, aquatint, woodcut.

The graphic process of printmaking lends itself to unique results of self-expression. Printmaking also allows designs to be reproduced. Printmaking is as much about the technique, from design through the process of printing, to final product, as it is about creativity.

Reading and Language Arts

Press: Look up a picture of a manual printing press in an encyclopedia. Enlarge the picture and label the press components.

Social Studies

Gutenberg: Do a unit study on Gutenberg and the invention of printing.

Math

Board game: Create a game using vegetable prints, which are a type of monoprint. Use dice to roll to move and practice adding.

Money Rub: You will need newsprint, tape, pencils and a sharpener, nickels, dimes, pennies, and quarters. Tape a coin to a flat surface with double stick tape. Place the newsprint over the coin and use the pencil to make a rubbing, Use several coins to create a design from the rubbings. Add up the amount of the coins used.

Science

Leaf Prints: Collect different types and sizes of leaves. You will also need newspaper, paint, paper, flat containers. Make prints by dipping the leaves in paint. Observe, compare, and describe the leaves. Identify and label parts on the leaf prints.

Music and Drama

Printed Drum: You will need empty round oatmeal containers, crayons, typing paper, wax paper, thick rubber bands, two corks, glue, two long pencils. Take the typing paper and make textural rubbings of bark, bricks, etc. Next, use vegetables and paint to print on the paper. Glue the paper around the outside of the oatmeal box. Cut a circle of wax paper larger than the diameter of the oatmeal box and secure it over the opening with a rubber band. To make drumsticks, twist pencils into the corks.

Culminating Activity

Screen Printing (Serigraphs): You need the following materials: embroidery hoop, stapler, cheese cloth large enough to fit over hoop, tag board, paper, scissors, finger paints, tongue depressor short enough to fit inside the hoop.

To make the "screen," stretch two layers of cheese cloth between the embroidery hoops. Cut a design from the tag board that will fit within the size of the hoop. This is the stencil. Put a piece of paper on the table and place the tag board stencil on top of it. Place the screen on top of the stencil. The cheesecloth should be against the paper and stencil. Drop some paint on to the screen inside the hoop. The finger paint should be about as thick as toothpaste. Hold the hoop down firmly with one hand and use the tongue depressor to scrape the paint across the stencil. Gently lift the stencil and hoop, making sure the stencil stays adhered to the cheese cloth. Repeat for more prints.

5

Fabric, Fiber, and Weaving

Examples of fabric, fiber, and weaving in picture books

Baker, Jeannie. *Window*. Greenwillow, 1991.

Birrer, Cynthia. *The Lady and the Unicorn*. Lothrop, Lee and Shepard, 1987. (Appliqué)

Blanco, Alberto. *The Desert Mermaid*. Children's Book Press, 1988. (Needlepoint)

Dorros, Arthur. *Tonight Is Carnival*. [Fabric work done by South American artists) Dutton, 1991. (Arpilleras)

Ehlert, Lois. *Moon Rope: Un Lazo la Luna*. Harcourt, Brace, Jovanovich, 1992. (Inspired by Peruvian textiles)

Heyer, Marilee. *The Weaving of a Dream*. Viking Kestrel, 1986. (Inspired by Chinese tapestry)

Mahy, Margaret. *17 Kings and 42 Elephants*. Dial, 1987. (Batik paintings on silk)

Richardson, Judith B. *The Way Home*. [Fabric work done by Salley Mavor] Macmillan, 1991. (Appliqué)

Roth, Susan L. *Gypsy Bird Song*. Harper Collins, 1991.

Towle, Faith M. *The Magic Cooking Pot*. Houghton Mifflin, 1975. (Indian batik)

Books about fabric, fiber, and weaving

Bingham, Caroline. *Crafts for Decoration*. Millbrook, 1993.

Deyrup, Astrith. *Tie Dyeing and Batik*. Doubleday, 1974.

Fitz-Gerald, Christina. *I Can Be a Textile Worker*. Children's Press, 1987.

Hindley, Judy. *A Piece of String Is a Wonderful Thing*. Candlewick, 1993.

Lancaster, John. *Fabric Art*. Franklin Watts, 1991.

Lohf, Sabine. *Things I Can Make with Cloth*. Chronicle Books, 1987.

O'Reilly, Susie. *Batik and Tie Dye*. Thompson Learning, 1993.

Solga, Kim. *Make Clothes Fun!* North Light Books, 1992.

Artists to Study

Moore, Reavis. *Native Artists of Africa*. John Muir, 1993.

Turner, Robyn. *Faith Ringgold*. Little Brown, 1993.

Objectives

1. To gain knowledge of the textile world, both past and present.
2. To discover how textiles are designed and manufactured.
3. To create an original mock batik design.

Related Vocabulary

Warp, weft, fiber, fabric, silk, tie-dye, batik, needlework, textile, silk.

Reading and Language Arts

Fabric Poem: Pass out scraps of different types, textures, and colors of fabric. Have the children write a descriptive poem that tells the color, pattern, texture, weight, type, and possible use of their scrap.

Social Studies

Fabric Around the Globe: Using the books *Crafts for Decoration* and *Batik and Tie Dye,* look at examples of fabrics that have been produced in different countries. Analyze the natural resources that were used in each case. Have pairs of students choose a country and research the native costume and fabric.

Math

Sequencing: Draw or obtain pictures of each step in making clothing from wool. Have the children practice sequencing them in the proper order. Include shearing, combing, spinning, weaving, designing, sewing, etc.

Science

Natural Dye Cooking: You will need white fabric, water, an old pan, a source of heat, and the materials listed below for desired colors. Boil the water in the old pan and add the chosen ingredient. Let the fabric soak for a minute. Remove the pan from the heat and allow the fabric to soak until the desired hue is achieved.

    Yellow—yellow onion skins
    Green— fresh spinach
    Purple—fresh blueberries
    Red—canned beets
    Blue—red cabbage
    Brown—tea leaves

Music and Drama

Streamer Sticks: Cut the cloth you dyed in the science activity into strips and attach a few of each color to a stick or dowel.

Use markers or crayons to put designs on the stick itself. Play music and practice making fiber designs in the air—snap your Streamer Stick, circle it, wave it, make a figure eight, and make free forms.

Culminating Activity

Black Glue Mock Batik: Materials: India ink, white clear drying glue, squeeze bottles, muslin white fabric, paintbrushes, bowls, acrylic paint.

Look over the book *17 Kings and 42 Elephants.* Discuss the design of the book and methods of batiking. Have each child design a batik on paper, keeping in mind that the end result of mock batik will look a little like stained glass. Designs should not be too intricate or detailed. Each child will mix a little India ink in a squeeze bottle with some white glue. Using the design they made as a guide, they will redraw it on the cloth using the ink/glue as the drawing tool. Let their designs dry completely. Thin the acrylic paints with water in the bowls. Each child now colors in the design using paint and brushes.

Fabric, fiber and weaving supplies

Rio Grande Weaving Supply
216 N. Pueblo Rd.
Taos, NM 97571

Earth Guild
One Tingle Alley, Dept T,
Asheville, NC 28801

6

Photography

Examples of photography in picture books

Ancona, George. *Handtalk Zoo*. Four Winds Press, 1989.

Doolittle, Eileen. *The Ark in the Attic*. [Pictures by Starr Ockenga] David R. Godine, 1987.

Henrietta. *A Mouse in the House*. Dorling Kindersley, 1991.

Hirschi, Ron. *A Time for Babies*. Cobblehill, 1993.

Hoban, Tana. *26 Letters and 99 Cents*. Greenwillow, 1987.

Izen, Marshall, and Jim West. *Why the Willow Weeps*. Delacorte, 1992.

Macmillan, Bruce. *Mouse Views: What the Class Pet Saw*. Holiday, 1993.

Wegman, William. *Cinderella*. Hyperion, 1993.

Wells, Ruth. *A to Zen: A Book of Japanese Culture*. Picture Book Studio, 1992.

Books about photography

Graham, Ian. *How It Works: Cameras*. Gloucester Press, 1991.

Jann, Gayle. *A Day in the Life of a Photographer*. Troll, 1988.

Morgan, Terri. *Photography: Take Your Best Shot*. Lerner, 1991.

Osinski, Christine. *I Can Be a Photographer*. Children's Press, 1986.

Artists to study

Adams, Ansel. *Ansel Adams: An Autobiography*. Little Brown, 1985.

Conrad, Pam. *Prairie Visions: The Life and Times of Solomon Butcher*. Harper Collins, 1991.

Mitchell, Barbara. *CLICK!* Carolrhoda, 1986. (George Eastman)

Siegel, Beatrice. *Eye on the World*. Warne, 1980. (Margaret Bourke-White)

Wolff, Sylvia. *Focus: Five Women Photographers*. Clarion, 1994. (Julia Cameron, Margaret Bourke-White, Flor Garduno, Sandy Skoglund, Lorna Simpson)

Objectives

1. Recognize photography as a technical skill and fine art.
2. Learn the basics of photography.

Related Vocabulary

Aperture, shutter, focus, film, lens, prism, speed.

Reading and Language Arts

Essay Cards: After looking at various photography books, make 3″ × 5″ cards with the steps involved in taking a photograph. The cards can be written or illustrated. Also make a diagram of a camera and label the parts.

Social Studies

Family Puppets: Cut up some old family photos which have good head shots. Cut the heads out of the photos. Now cut clothes and bodies from old magazines. Glue the heads from the family photos to the clothes. Tape the figure to a stick. Improvise a puppet show with your new family puppets.

Math

Camera Math: The diaphragm and the f-stop on a camera make a good starting point for a discussion on higher and lower numbers and sizes. The higher the f-stop, the smaller the aperture size becomes. The aperture size also affects the depth of field: the smaller the aperture, the larger the depth of field. For example, if something were close to the camera, the f-stop would be low (F2). If something is far away, the f-stop would be higher (F16).

Science

Science Photography: Use the book *Fun and Games: Stories Science Photos Tell* (Lothrop, 1991). Pick a photo from the book and do a study of its concept. Included are photos of the atmosphere, gravity, sound waves, and x-ray waves. Do a comparison of the camera and the human eye.

Flower Photo Hunt: Gather up several books that have photographs of wildflowers. Some to use are *Counting Wildflowers*. Bruce Macmillan (Lothrop, 1986); *Flowers, Fruits, and Seeds*. Jerome Wexler (Prentice-Hall, 1986); and *Roses Red, Violets Blue*. Sylvia Johnson (Lerner, 1991). Have the children locate or identify as many of the photos as they can. Take a polaroid and photograph some wildflowers found in your area.

Music and Drama

World Stories: Dramatize an original story written by your group to go with a photo from the book *Eye On the World*.

Culminating Activity

Pinhole Camera: Using a medium-size cardboard box, poke a tiny hole with a needle on one side. On the other side cut out a large square and cover the hole with white tissue paper. In a darkened room, if a flashlight is placed against the pinhole, an image of the flashlight bulb filament will appear on the tissue. Place some blueprint paper in the box over the tissue and develop a print of the filament as described in the Robot City activity.

7

Collage

Examples of collage in picture books

Brisson, Pat. *Benny's Pennies*. [Illustrations by Bob Barner] Doubleday, 1983.

Bunting, Eve. *Smoky Night*. [Illustrations by David Diaz] Harcourt Brace Jovanovich, 1994.

Ehlert, Lois. *Red Leaf, Yellow Leaf*. HBJ, 1991.

Fleming, Denise. *Lunch*. Henry Holt, 1992.

Fox, Mem. *Shoes from Grandpa*. Orchard, 1988.

Hol, Coby. *A Visit to the Farm*. North South, 1989.

Johnston, Tony. *The Old Lady and The Bird*. [Pictures by Stephanie Garcia] Philomel, 1994.

Kingsland, Robin. *Bus Stop Bop*. [Pictures by Alex Ayliffe] Viking, 1991.

Lear, Edward. *A Was Once an Apple Pie*. [Pictures by Julie Lacome] Candlewick Press, 1992.

Lionni, Leo. *Mr. McMouse*. Knopf, 1992.

MacDonald, Suse. *Space Spinners*. Dial, 1991.

Patterson, Bettina. *In My Yard*. Holt, 1992.

Wisniewski, David. *Rain Player*. Clarion, 1991.

Books about collage

Boutan, Mila. *Collages*. WJ Fantasy Books, 1992.

Corwin, Judith Hoffman. *Papercrafts*. Franklin Watts, 1988.

Devonshire, Hillary. *Collage*. Watts, 1988.

Guerrier, Charlie. *A Collage of Crafts*. Ticknor and Fields, 1994.

Tofts, Hannah. *The Collage Book*. Simon and Schuster, 1991.

Artists to study

Brust, Beth. *The Amazing Paper Cuttings of Hans Christian Andersen*. Ticknor and Fields, 1993.

Cain, Micheal. *Louise Nevelson*. Chelsea House, 1989.

Carle, Eric. *The Art of Eric Carle*. Picture Book Studio, 1993.

Objectives

1. Improve cutting, gluing, arranging and assembling skills.
2. Learn the different materials used in collage.

Related Vocabulary

Collage, assemblage, montage, awl, sampler.

Reading and Language Arts

Matching Collage: Make collages of pictures of matching word sets. Use drawings or pictures cut from magazines. Some examples: Bread and _____, Shoes and _____, Tree and _____. Be sure to have the children label their collages.

Social Studies

Giant Collage: As a group, decide a theme for a giant collage. Before you begin to make the art, vote on what materials, colors, patterns, and design will be included. Assemble the collage and visit local organizations to check if they have an area where you can display your cooperative effort. (Try the public library, school, church, bank, or a parent's office.)

Math

Fraction Collages: Cut out pictures from old magazines. Cut the pictures in the following fractions: 1/2, 1/4, 1/3, 1/6, etc. Have the children then glue the pictures on paper in a design they like. Collages can also be made from geometric shapes which can be sorted and counted by shape and color.

Science

Hot Collage: Discuss the concepts of hot and cold. The children can then make a "Hot Collage." Arrange sequins, plastic, glitter, and tinsel inside a plastic sandwich bag . When the design is ready, slip the plastic bag between two pieces of aluminum foil. Press a warm iron on the foil for about 15 seconds. The heat will melt the plastic and hold the collage pieces in place.

Rock Mosaic: Show the children examples of mosaic, which is a collage made up of tiles or stone. Do an observation and collection walk, gathering up and sorting rocks. Classify the rocks by color, texture, kind, and size. Now make rock mosaics by gluing the found rocks on to a margarine tub lid with white glue.

Music and Drama

Collage Shaker: For this activity, gather up discarded 6″ foil pie tins, masking tape, glue, colored pasta in different shapes and sizes, and dried beans. Drop a few dried beans in a foil pan. Place another pan on top of it and tape the pans together with masking tape to make a shaker. Use glue to attach the colored pasta in a collage pattern or design on both sides of the shakers. Dance and shake your collage shaker to music.

Culminating Activity

Memory Box: The next time a trip is taken, children can collect small interesting objects to make a memory collage in a box. Pictures, postcards, souvenirs, and nature items work well. Use a small shoe box or cigar box with the top removed. The sides of the box will serve as a "frame" to the collage. Make a background on the inside bottom of the box using paint, a map, or travel brochure. Arrange your objects as desired, and attach with glue, tape, or pins.

8

Architecture

Examples of architecture in picture books

Barton, Byron. *Building a House*. Greenwillow, 1991.

Chetwin, Grace. *Mr. Meredith and the Truly Remarkable Stone*. Bradbury, 1989.

Chorao, Kay. *Cathedral Mouse*. Dutton, 1988.

Crosbie, Michael, and Steve Rosenthal. *Architecture Shapes*. Preservation Press, 1993.

Gibbons, Gail. *How a House Is Built*. Holiday, 1990.

———. *Up Goes the Skyscraper!* Four Winds, 1986.

Giblin, James Cross. *The Skyscraper Book*. Little Brown, 1981.

Ichikawa, Satomi. *Nora's Castle*. Philomel, 1986.

Books about architecture

Biesty, Stephen. *Stephen Biesty's Incredible Cross Sections*. Knopf, 1992.

Clinton, Susan. *I Can Be an Architect*. Children's Press, 1986.

Darling, David. *Spider Webs to Sky Scrapers*. Macmillan, 1991.

Dunn, Andrew. *Skyscrapers*. Thompson Learning, 1993.

Hogner, Franz. *From Blueprint to House*. Carolrhoda, 1986.

Isaacson, Philip. *Round Buildings, Square Buildings, Buildings that Wiggle Like a Fish*. Knopf, 1988.

The Visual Dictionary of Buildings. Dorling Kindersley, 1992.

Wilkinson, Phil. *Amazing Buildings*. Dorling Kindersley, 1992.

Artists to Study

Hudson, Karen. *The Will and the Way*. Rizzoli, 1994. (Paul R. Williams)

Thorne-Thomasen, Kathleen. *Frank Lloyd Wright for Kids*. Chicago Review, 1994.

Wadsworth, Ginger. *Julia Morgan: Architect of Dreams*. Lerner, 1990.

Objectives

1. Become familiar with architectural shapes and forms.
2. Identify a few major architectural styles.
3. Practice fine detail and design skills.

Related Vocabulary

Form, massing, ornamentation, construction, plan, porch, galleria, portico, gable, gambrel, mansard.

Reading and Language Arts

Architectural Friend: Have each child pick out an interesting building or structure from your community, such as the courthouse, a home, a landmark, etc. Have them research and find out when it was built, who built it, and the history of the building. If your community is lacking in such structures, choose famous buildings, such as the Sistine Chapel.

Social Studies

Architecture Treasure Hunt: Identify the different parts of local buildings using a fill-in sheet with a drawing of the structure. Have kids label the roof, columns, windows, and identify the materials, surface treatment, and other architectural details.

Dream House: The only limitation on this project is the child's imagination. Have them design a floorplan for their dream structure. It could be a house, school, library, playhouse, or anything else they would like. Be sure to include details such as placement of plugs, doors, windows, vents, etc.

Math

Toothpick Building: Using toothpicks and small balls of gray clay, each child can design and build an architectural structure. When completed, measure one toothpick and calculate the height, width, perimeter, etc. of their buildings.

Science

Animal Architecture: Use any of the following books to do a study on animals habitations:

    Animal Architecture. National Geographic, 1990.

    Dewey, Jennifer. *Animal Architecture.* Orchard, 1991.

    Forsyth, Adrian. *The Architecture of Animals.* Cambden, 1989.

    Kitchen, Bert. *And So They Build.* Candlewick, 1993.

    Pringle, Lawrence. *Home.* Macmillan, 1987.

Music and Drama

Hansel's House: Find a recording of the opera "Hansel and Gretel" by Englebert Humperdinck. Listen to the opera. Give the children graham crackers, cream cheese thinned with milk, cookies, candies, and cereal. Using the thinned cream cheese as mortar, they can create graham cracker cabins as inspired by the music.

Culminating Activity

Pyramid: Share the book *Pyramid* by David Macaulay. Discuss the way the pyramid might have actually been constructed and how they could have done the planning for it. Construct your own pyramid using an 8–1/2″ square sheet of heavy paper. Fold the right corner down to the lower left to form a triangle. Open and fold the left corner in the same manner. Cut one fold line to the center of the square. Overlap two of the triangles and glue together to form a pyramid. Decorate the pyramids. Fasten them to cardboard to create an Egyptian city.

Architectural Information
American Architectural Foundation
1735 New York Ave NW
Washington, DC 20006
1-800-242-4140

Bibliography

Amabile, Teresa. *Growing Up Creative: A Lifetime of Creativity*. Creative Education Foundation, 1992.

Art Enrichment: How to Implement a Museum/School Program. University of Texas at Austin, 1980.

Association for Childhood Education International. "The Child's Right to The Expressive Arts: Nurturing Imagination as Well as Intellect." *Childhood Education* 66, 195–201.

Blizzard, Gladys. *A Child's Book of Art: Great Pictures*. Dorling Kindersley, 1994.

———. *Come Look with Me: Enjoying Art with Children*. Thomasson Grant, 1991.

———. *Come Look with Me: Exploring Landscape Art with Children*. Thomasson Grant, 1991.

———. *Worlds of Play*. Thomasson Grant, 1993.

Bolton, Linda. *Hidden Pictures*. Dial, 1993.

Brittain, W. L. *Creativity, Art, and the Young Child*. Macmillan, 1979.

Broudy, H.S. "Why Art in Education and Why Art Education?" In *Beyond Creating: The Place for Art in America's Schools*. Getty Center for Education in the Arts, 1985.

Cane, F. *The Artist in Each of Us*. Art Therapy Publications, 1983.

Chapman, L. *Approaches to Art in Education*. HBJ, 1978.

"Characteristics List." *Project Art Band: A Program for Visually Gifted Children*. DeCordova Museum, 1982.

Cole, Alison. *Perspective*. Dorling Kindersley, 1993.

Corwin, S. "Reading Improvement Through Art: Success Story from the Big Apple." *School Arts*. (January 1977): 52–55.

Davidson, Rosemary. *Take a Look: An Introduction into the Experience of Art*. Viking, 1993.

Day, Barbara. *Early Childhood Education: Creative Learning Activities*. Macmillan, 1983.

Dimondstein, Geraldine. *Exploring the Arts with Children*. Macmillan, 1974.

Discipline Based Art Education: What Form Will It Take? Getty Center for the Arts in Education, 1987.

Dobbs, S., H. Feinstein, and R. MacGregor. *Research Readings for Discipline Based Art Education*. National Art Education Association, 1988.

Duke, L.L. "The Getty Center for Education in the Arts," *Art Education,* 36(5): 4–8.

Ellison, R., et al. "Using Biographical Information in Identifying Artistic Talent." In *Psychology and Education of the Gifted* edited by W. Barbe and J. Renzulli. Irvington Publishers, 1975.

Ellsworth, M., and M. Andrews. *Growing with Art: A Teacher's Book*. Singer Company, 1960.

Frost, Joanne. *Art, Books, and Children: Art Activities Based on Children's Literature*. Special Literature Press, 1984.

Gardener, J. *Henry Moore: From Bones and Stones to Sketches and Sculpture.* Four Winds, 1993.

Goodman, Kenneth. *What's Whole in Whole Language?* Heinemann Educational Books, 1986.

Greenberg, Jan. *The Painter's Eye.* Doubleday, 1991.

———. *The Sculptor's Eye.* Doubleday, 1993.

Greer, W. D. "Discipline Based Art Education: Approaching Art as a Subject of Study." *Studies in Art Education,* 25(4): 212–218.

Hardiman, G. and Zernich, T. *Art Activities for Children.* Prentice Hall, 1981

Hess, Robert, and Doreen Croft. *Teachers of Young Children.* Houghton Mifflin, 1972.

Hoffman, Suzanne, and Linda L. Lamme. *Learning from the Inside Out: The Expressive Arts.* Association for Childhood Education International, 1989.

Isaacson, Philip. *A Short Walk Around the Pyramids and Through the World of Art.* Alfred A. Knopf, 1993.

Kaufman, M. "The Book as Art and Idea." *Art Education,* 36(3): 40–46.

Knox, Bob. *The Great Art Adventure.* Rizzoli, 1993.

Lansing, Kenneth. "The Research of Jean Piaget and Its Implications for Art Education in the Elementary School." *Studies in Art Education,* vol. 7, no. 2 (1966): 35–38.

Laughlin, Mildred K., and Terri Street, eds. *Literature Based Art and Music: Children's Books and Activities to Enrich the K–5 Curriculum.* Oryx Press, 1992.

Lindernam, E. *Developing Artistic and Perceptual Awareness*. William C. Brown, 1981.

Lowenfeld, Viktor, and W. Lambert Brittan. *Creative and Mental Growth*. Macmillan, 1982.

MacCaulay, David. *Black and White*. Houghton, 1990.

MacClintock, D. *Animals Observed: A Look at Animals in Art*. Charles Scribner, 1993.

Marantz, K. "On the Mysteries of Reading and Art: The Picture Book as Art Object." In *Reading, the Arts and the Creation of Meaning,* edited by E. Eisner, 71–89. National Art Education Association, 1978.

Marantz, Sylvia. *Picture Books for Looking & Learning: Wakening Visual Perceptions Through the Art of Children's Books, Preschool–6th Grade*. Oryx Press, 1992.

McHugh, Christopher. "Exploring Art Series." Thompson Learning, 1993. (Animals, Faces, Food, People at Work, Town and Country)

Micklethwaite, Lucy. *A Child's Book of Art: Great Pictures, First Words*. Dorling Kindersley, 1993.

———. *I Spy with Two Eyes: Numbers in Art*. Greenwillow, 1993.

Neal, Judith C. "The Very Hungry Caterpillar Meets Beowulf in the Secondary Classroom." *Journal of Reading,* 35:4 (December 1991).

Parnall, Peter. *Spaces*. Millbrook, 1993.

Richardson, Joy. *Inside the Museum: A Child's Guide to the Metropolitan Museum of Art*. Abrams, 1993.

Scholler, Ruth, et al. "Reading Enrichment Art Devlopment." *School Arts*. (January 1983): 40–41.

Seely, C., and Hurwitz, A. "Developing Language Through Art," *School Arts*. (May 1983): 20–21.

Talking with Artists. Bradbury, 1992.

Taylor, Anne. *Math in Art*. Activity Resources Press, P.O. Box 4875, Hayward, CA 94540, 1974.

Woolf, Felicity. *Picture This: A First Introduction to Painting*. Doubleday, 1991.

Yenawine, Philip. *Colors*. Delacorte/MOMA, 1991.

———. *Lines*. Delacorte/MOMA, 1991.

———. *People*. Delacorte/MOMA, 1993.

———. *Shapes*. Delacorte/MOMA, 1991.

———. *Stories*. Delacorte/MOMA, 1991.

Zucker, Barbara F. *Children's Museums, Zoos, and Discovery Centers: An International Reference Guide*. Greenwood Publishing Group, 1987.

Material Resources

Insect Lore Products
P.O. Box 1535
Shafter, CA 93263
1-805-746-6047

Butterfly Garden Kit

Crystal Productions
Art Education Resouces Catalog
Box 2159
Glenview, IL 60025
1-800-255-8629

Catalog of all media types on art skills, appreciation, multi-cultural art, careers, and crafts.

NewsCurrents
P.O. Box 52-CCTT
Madison, WI 53791–9483
1-800-356-2303

Catalog of art appreciation/art history posters, prints, and videos.

Carolina Biological Supply
Burlington, NC
1-800-334-5551

Raise A Butterfly Kit

General Index

Index of Authors

Index of Titles

About the Author

Robin Works Davis is the Youth Services Librarian at the Hurst Public Library in Hurst, Texas. She formerly worked in the Children's Department of the Richardson Public Library. She obtained her Bachelor of Fine Arts degree from Baylor University and her Masters in Library and Information Science from the University of North Texas. She is a member of the Texas Library Association, American Library Association, International Reading Association, and Kappa Delta Sorority Alumni Association. In 1993 she recieved the ALSC/Book Wholesalers National Reading Program Grant. Ms. Davis has also done extensive consulting on children's programming and literature. She is the author of two reading club manuals for the State of Texas, *Creature Features* (Texas State Library, 1989) and *Camp Wanna-Read* (Texas State Library, 1991). She is also the author of *Promoting Reading through Reading Programs* (Neal Schuman, 1992) and *An Alphabet of Books* (Highsmith Press, 1994).